A HANDWEAVER'S
WORKBOOK

The four-harness loom (counterbalanced and nonfolding or rigid type). A. Breast beam. B. Cloth beam. C. Treadles. D. Top of beater or handtree. E. Reed. F. Lamms (4). G. Harnesses (4). H. Slabstock. I. Warp beam. J. Lower horizontal bars (4). K. Heddles. L. Crank. M. Corner posts. N. Upper side bars (2). O. Ratchets, front and rear (this loom has a friction brake on warp beam not visible in the photo). P. Handle on front ratchet dog. Q. Pedal on rear brake. R. Loom uprights. S. Sides or swords of beater. T. Lower bar of the beater. U. Small rollers (2). V. Large roller. W. Slot for insertion of large roller. X. Point where lamms are attached. Y. Weaving capacity of the loom. Z. Point where beater is attached. *This loom is manufactured by Nilus LeClerc, Inc., L'Isletville, Quebec, Canada. Photograph by Charles E. Simmons.*

A HANDWEAVER'S WORKBOOK

HEATHER G. THORPE

COLLIER BOOKS

A Division of Macmillan Publishing Co., Inc.

NEW YORK

COLLIER MACMILLAN PUBLISHERS

LONDON

Macmillan Publishing Co., Inc.
866 Third Avenue, New York, N.Y. 10022
Collier-Macmillan Canada Ltd.

A Handweaver's Workbook is published in a hardcover
edition by Macmillan Publishing Co., Inc.

Library of Congress Catalog Card Number: 56-7668

First Collier Books Edition 1974

Second Printing 1975

Printed in the United States of America

To my instructor, Rupert Peters, whose generous sharing made this book possible.

FOREWORD

A Handweaver's Workbook is made up of two parts. Part
One concerns itself with the four-harness loom and how it is assem-
bled and with the various processes which constitute the preparation, beaming, threading, sleying, and weaving of a warp. It is intended for beginners and, consequently, is written in considerable
detail. In this mass of information, more experienced weavers may,
however, find some ideas which they also can use.

Part Two deals with some of the weaves for a four-harness loom.
Weaves are not the same as weaving drafts but are the particular
methods of threading the warp which introduce new principles into
the construction of the woven fabric or into the forming of patterns. (Zielinski: *Encyclopedia of Weaving.*) Part Two is for the
weaver who is not content to be a mere "shuttle-pusher," but who
wishes to know what happens, when, and why. If you are such a
weaver, you have arrived at the point where this part of the book
will be of interest to you.

Avail yourself also of the many other texts on weaving, a few of
which are mentioned in the Bibliography.

A Handweaver's Workbook is devoted entirely to a discussion of
the four-harness loom, whether it is a floor loom or a table loom.
It does not take up the subject of the operation of a loom equipped
with a fly shuttle, although the preparation of such a loom for
weaving is largely the same. Two-harness looms and looms having
more than four harnesses are also dressed in the same way as described in Part One.

At this time, I wish to express my thanks to all my weaving students of the Buffalo Museum of Science and of the University of Buffalo who have, willy-nilly, been my most helpful guinea pigs.

Heather G. Thorpe

Buffalo, New York
February, 1956

CONTENTS

ix

God loveth sinners,
Dyers and spinners,
Weavers even
May hope for Heaven.
When naught is left
Of warp and weft,
With spindle and loom
They will meet their Doom;
The Lamb's white fleece
Has bought their peace.

HILARY PEPLER

*Reprinted by kind permission of
Ditchling Press, Limited.*

PART ONE

THE FOUR-HARNESS LOOM

Notes on Winding, Beaming, Threading,
Sleying, and Weaving a Warp

Chapter 1

THE FOUR-HARNESS LOOM

All weaving is done by means of a loom of some kind. It may be the fingers alone that form the loom. It may be only a simple frame upon which threads are strung, and over and under which the weaver works a needle in a process similar to darning. The loom with which *A Handweaver's Workbook* is concerned, however, is a far cry from such simple appliances, for each part of it is precision built for the function it is to perform.

The frontispiece shows a four-harness floor loom, the term *four-harness* referring to the number of rectangular frames called *harnesses* which it has and which are marked (G) in the picture. Harnesses are essential to a loom of this type, for it is by means of them that patterns are woven in the material. Many looms are built which have only two harnesses, and on them many lovely effects can be obtained by the introduction of color in the threads used, by the use of various fibers, and by following certain "two-harness techniques" with which this book is not concerned. The four-harness loom, however, is capable of producing all these effects, and in addition the owner of such a loom has at his or her command thousands of other beautiful patterns from which to choose. Indeed, the more harnesses a loom has, the more complicated it becomes. There are weavers who prefer to delve into the intricacies of the eight-, twelve-, and even sixteen-harness looms. But for the beginner four harnesses are ample. Indeed, they are a challenge to the skill, artistic ability, and imagination of even the most experienced weaver.

There are many things that have to be taken into consideration by a person who is about to purchase a loom which can be matters of personal preference rather than of the loom's performance. Therefore, let us first find out what a more or less average four-harness loom is like and then discuss later various other types of four-harness looms available.

PARTS OF THE LOOM

Let us suppose that your loom has arrived from the factory, and that it is of the type shown in the frontispiece. Upon arrival a loom is often in a knocked-down or partly knocked-down condition. Therefore, upon opening the cartons or boxes, check their contents against the illustration given in the loom catalog or against the one in this book. Take care also to shake out all paper or other packing material, for small parts are easily overlooked. Read any instructions which have been included carefully. It is wise also to lay each separate loom part out on the floor where they can all be studied. Here, in addition to the four harnesses, is what you should find:

1. The makings of a framework: four vertical and eight horizontal bars. Two of the horizontal ones are known as the *breast beam* (A) and the *slabstock* (H). Four (J) form the lower supports for the four vertical posts (M). Of these the one along the front of the loom is referred to as the *heel bar*. The other two horizontal bars (N) will strengthen the framework at the sides.

2. A set of four or six *treadles,* depending upon the make of your loom (C).

3. Two large beams. One is the *cloth beam* (B), the other one the *warp beam* (I). These are equipped with toothed *ratchets* (O) which have catches called *pawls* or *dogs*. The catch on the cloth

beam usually has a long handle as at (P). On the warp beam (I) the catch has a long pedal extending to the heel bar as at (Q) or a long handle. (See Glossary: *Friction Brake.*)

4. Two side pieces or loom uprights (R). There may also be a horizontal bar which caps these side pieces which the loom pictured does not have.

5. A *beater* or *batten*. This consists of four parts, two side pieces called *swords* (S), a top bar (D) called the *handtree* and a lower transverse bar (T) which is permanently fixed to the swords. The top bar (D) is removable and usually is fastened in place by wing nuts.

6. One *reed* (E) having steel partitions. The reed may or may not be already fitted into the grooved upper and lower transverse parts of the beater.

7. A set of four short levers called *lamms* (F) hinged at one end or with a hole bored through the end of each one and a rod put through them.

8. Three rollers much smaller in circumference than the cloth and warp beams. Two of these rollers (U) are smaller and shorter than the other one (V). These are for the suspension of the harnesses, and they usually have hooks at each end where cords can be fastened for this purpose.

9. Several hundred needle-like *heddles* of twisted or flat steel wire (K). They are slotted at the ends and have eyes in the middle through which threads called *warp ends* are put when the loom is readied for weaving later on. These heddles may or may not be found already strung upon narrow steel bars on the harnesses when the loom arrives.

10. Various bolts, screws, nuts, washers, the crank (L), and perhaps even a wrench. Also a hank of cord or ready-cut cords. Cord is used for tying up the three rollers, the harnesses, the lamms, and the treadles, though on some looms webbing or link chain is used for this purpose.

11. Two large pieces of canvas, strong cotton or ticking called *aprons*. These are often found already tacked along the cloth

and warp beams of floor looms. They are needed when the loom is being prepared for weaving. Some looms substitute long cords for aprons.

12. Two very smooth, flat sticks about one inch wide, as long as the large beams of your loom and having a hole bored at each end. They are called *lease* (or *leash*) *sticks*. Two more sticks or sometimes metal rods are called *apron sticks*. These latter are slipped through the cords or hems of the aprons. Lease sticks do not fit anywhere into the loom but are needed later.

13. *Shuttles* to carry the thread used when weaving. Most manufacturers supply one boat shuttle at least, see Illustration 25 on page 89. One shuttle is not enough for most four-harness weaving, and it would be a good thing for weavers to insist that a pair of shuttles be included in the price of the loom.

14. A *draw-in* or *reed hook,* see Illustration 12 on page 50. This, too, will not be needed right now.

ASSEMBLING THE LOOM

Now you are ready to assemble your loom. The holes for the insertion of bolts and screws are bored at the factory so the assembly is not difficult. Unless the loom is an exceptionally large and heavy one, like the old timers made of hand-hewn logs, a woman can do the assembling alone. The assistance of another pair of hands is, however, usually gratefully received when the time comes to hang the rollers and the harnesses. The following is the procedure I have found best to use:

1. Assemble the two sides of the loom's framework by fastening to the corner posts (M) the lower side horizontal bars (J) at floor level, and the two upper side pieces (N). Most looms today are fastened together by the use of bolts, making a very rigid construction. Looms of the older type may have what are called tenons, or projecting parts left in the ends of the frame by cutting the wood away from around them. Each tenon fits into a mortise to make a joint. When the tenons extend right

through the mortise, the joint is made secure by the insertion of a wedge.

2. Insert the warp beam (I) into the holes in the two rear posts, and see that the pedal (Q) which is used to release the tension on the warp beam, is also in place at the right side of the loom at the floor. On looms where the tension is released on this beam from the front by hand, there will be a long handle on the catch or brake instead of a pedal.

3. The cloth beam (B) complete with ratchet and its long-handled catch (P) is now slipped into the holes bored, or slots made, in the side pieces (N) near the front of the loom. The advantage of having slots rather than holes here is to permit the removal of the cloth beam when the loom is being threaded. This gives more room in which to work.

4. Fasten the heel bar (J) in front and the rear bar (J) to the corner posts.

5. Unfasten the top horizontal bar on the beater (D), and place the reed in the grooves made to receive it. New reeds are oily so clean yours with a carbon tetrachloride spot remover using a brush to get between the steel partitions. Refasten the top (handtree) and secure the entire beater to the lower side of the loom at the outside as at (Z). The beater is not rigidly fastened into the frame of the loom for it must swing back and forth between the breast beam and the harnesses (G). On the other hand, it must not wobble from side to side. It must also be in alignment, for if a beater is warped out of shape, it is useless. The beater is that part of the loom which beats the material being woven into place, and for this reason it must strike the last row of weaving squarely across the width of it.

6. The tall upright side pieces of the loom (R) are now attached to the side frames of the loom. The framework of the entire loom and these two uprights must be very rigid so all bolts must be fastened securely. The uprights must also be absolutely perpendicular or the harnesses will not hang properly.

7. Now the breast beam (A) and the slabstock (H) can be slipped

over the tops of the corner posts. These two horizontal bars are not bolted or fastened securely in place as a rule because it is often desirable to remove them.

8. At either the right or the left side of the loom on the inside of the frame you will see a place where the lamms (F) are to be fastened. See (X) on the frontispiece. With the lamms there may be furnished washers or small wooden "doughnuts" which are to hold the four lamms apart so they will not rub one against the other. On that surface of each lamm which is to be placed toward the floor, there is a row of screw eyes or hooks. The upper side is the one with a single screw eye or hook in it, where it will later be fastened to the harness which is directly above. The lamms are hinged at the end next to the framework so that, until they are tied up or hooked up by and by, they will fall down to the floor. It is immaterial whether the lamms are fastened at the left side or the right side of the frame as long as you follow the manufacturer's plan.

9. Bolt on the treadles (C) to either the heel bar (J in front) or the back bar (J) depending upon whether they are supposed to be attached in front or at the rear of the loom. Your catalog will show you this. Most floor looms with four harnesses have six treadles, but some have only four. My preference is for the ones with six treadles but, inasmuch as you can weave identically on a loom which has either four or six treadles, the question is largely one of opinion. Because the treadles are hinged at the point of attachment, they, like the lamms, will drop down to the floor until they are later tied up. Sometimes the treadles are attached to the loom when it arrives and it is just wonderful, too, if they are all tied up as shown in the frontispiece.

10. If the heddles (K) are not already placed on the narrow flat metal bars as seen in the frontispiece, divide their number (at least for now) evenly among the four harnesses. The metal bars are removable to facilitate this process. Do not bother to thread

each heddle separately for this takes too much time. Instead, slip them one after the other off the cord, upon which they are strung, onto these metal bars. The heddles have slots at top and bottom through which these bars go. Just be careful not to twist one heddle over the other as this is being done. Wire heddles are alike at top and bottom, but the flat steel heddles have a crimped slot at one end and a plain one at the other. Place the crimped slot on the upper bars of each harness and then all the eyes of the heddles will be in the position most suitable for threading them. It will not do to have some of them turned one way and some the other, and they must be the same on all four harnesses. The upper part of the harness is the one having a hook at each end. When all heddles are on the bars, replace them in the harnesses, and snap the springs which hold the bars in place.

11. The largest of the three remaining rollers is now placed in a horizontal position so that the ends of it rest in the holes or slots found in the tall uprights of the loom at or near the top (W). This roller turns freely back and forth. If the loom has a top bar, it is also put in place at this time. The loom illustrated has none.

12. The two smaller rollers (U) are now hung from this larger roller by means of two cords, one around each end of it. The smaller rollers are furnished with hooks or some other device into which these cords fasten. Many manufacturers today are very helpful and supply cords just the needed length and with loops fashioned in them for the insertion of the hooks of the smaller rollers. We will take for granted that your loom has this convenient feature and then later go into details about what to do if you have to cut your own cord lengths.

Wind each cord, therefore, one and a half times around the large roller, placing each cord about one inch in from the end. Here it helps to have another person hold these cords to prevent them from unwinding.

13. The looped ends of the cords which are hanging down from the front of this roller are caught into the end hooks of one of the smaller rollers. The back loops are caught into the hooks of the second small roller. See (a) and (b) of Illustration 1 which shows an end-on view of the rollers and their cords. When you have completed this step, you will have one roller at the top of the loom and hanging from it two smaller ones which should now be adjusted until they are horizontal. The hooks in the ends of each small roller are made so that they swivel, and therefore these rollers move freely.

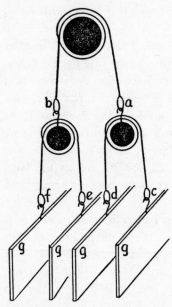

Illustration 1. End view shows the suspension of harnesses by means of the rollers. These cords are ready-made to size.

14. The time has come to hang the harnesses. Take two more cords and wind them one and a half turns around one of the small rollers placing one cord at or near each end of it. Then while your helper holds the two small rollers, loop the front ends of these cords (c) into the hooks of one of the harnesses and then take another harness and do the same with the rear loops of these cords as at (d). The harnesses (g), being all alike, it makes no difference which you use first. The other two harnesses are connected to the other small roller in the same manner as indicated at (e) and (f). Push down on all four harnesses at the same time, and presently they will all be hanging evenly.

15. As you can see, the harnesses are hanging free at the bottom, and now they are to be attached to the lamms underneath them one by one. The harness in front (the one next to the

beater) is called harness number one, and it is attached to the lamm underneath, which is nearest the front of the loom. The next harness, number two, is attached to the next lamm and so on for all four harnesses and lamms. Better type looms have V-shaped steel wire pieces at the bottom of each harness which catch into a hook on the top of each lamm. The V-shape of this wire keeps the harnesses horizontal when they are in use. When all four harnesses are fastened to the lamms, the latter should be horizontal with respect to the floor, and harnesses and rollers should be level as seen in the illustration of the four-harness loom.

ATTACHING ROLLERS AND HARNESSES

If the manufacturer of your loom has not supplied you with ready-made cords for the attachment of the rollers and harnesses, you will of course be obliged to cut them yourself from the hank of cord provided. An old loom which you have resurrected from somewhere will also have to have its new cords cut to size. It is a tricky thing to get the harnesses just the right height from the top of the loom so that the weaving will be satisfactory. In general, however, on a loom of this type they should hang so that when a lightweight cord is tied from the slabstock and threaded through the eye of one of the heddles and then through one of the slots called *dents* in the reed and finally tied to the breast beam, it will be horizontal. In order to accomplish this, it will be necessary to cut the cords for the suspension of the rollers and harnesses long enough so that they can be adjusted up or down. This final adjustment of the cords is made after the loom is all threaded and ready for weaving.

On page 76, there is shown the *snitch* or *loom* knot which is the one used when cords are to be made adjustable. In order to hang the two smaller rollers from the larger one, double two long pieces of your cord, making them long enough to go around the upper roller one and a half times with both the looped and the cut ends hanging down. As the rollers are tied the same at each end, Illustration 2 shows an end-on view of them. Take one of the long doubled

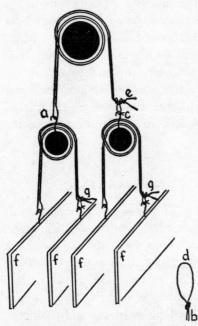

pieces and, after winding it one and a half times around the big roller, fasten the looped end into the hook of the small roller as at (a). You will be glad of an assistant to hold the roller for you. Just how long to make the hanging ends of the cord is difficult to say for it depends upon the height of the top roller, but eight to ten inches will usually suffice.

Next take a shorter length of cord and knot it into a loop about six inches long (b). Attach this loop to the hook of the other small roller as at (c). Have the knot come near the hook. Then by bending the loop at (d) back upon itself the cut ends hanging down from the upper roller are tied at (e) in a snitch knot by following the steps in Illustration

Illustration 2. End view of the rollers. These cords have been cut and snitch knots used.

21. The distance from the top of the large roller to the top of the small rollers after the snitch knots at (e) are tied and adjusted will be somewhere between eight and ten inches unless the loom you have has extremely high side uprights.

In Illustration 2 you can see that the harnesses (f) are attached in pairs to each small roller in the same manner by doubled cords, loops, and snitch knots. When these cords have been tied, adjust the snitch knots at (g) for the time being so that the eyes in the heddles are in line with the top of the breast beam and the slabstock as was described on page 11. On my looms the distance from the top of small rollers to the top of the harnesses is less than that from the large roller to the small rollers or about six inches. The rollers and harnesses should be horizontal and level.

If there are no V-shaped wire pieces or any hooks on the bottom of the harnesses for attaching them to the lamms, you will have to tie snitch knots here, too. Loop a doubled strand of cord around the bottom of each harness exactly in the center. The ends of a similarly doubled cord coming from the lamm directly beneath the harness are used to complete the knot. When adjusted the four lamms should be horizontal in respect to the floor and all level. Of course, all three rollers and the four harnesses must also be horizontal.

WHAT STYLE OF LOOM TO CHOOSE

There is a great difference of opinion among weavers concerning the best type of loom to own. A loom is often a lifetime investment involving considerable outlay of money, therefore it pays to investigate carefully before buying. There are guilds and periodicals devoted to weaving mentioned in the Bibliography from which you can get good advice to form your own conclusions. I recommend especially that you look over the advertisements and pertinent articles in the *Handweaver & Craftsman,* a quarterly which no weaver can afford to be without. Check carefully the manufacturers' specifications, their guarantees, what they supply with the loom in the way of aprons and shuttles, delivery charges, etc.

The question of the size of loom to purchase is one of great importance to a new weaver. To weave wide materials, such as draperies and coverlets, you will require a loom which has a weaving capacity of 45 inches at least. The weaving capacity of a loom is determined by the width of the harnesses (see Y on the frontispiece). For suiting and other yardages one of the 36-inch looms will be wide enough. There are also floor looms which are narrower, weaving from about sixteen to twenty-seven inches. But in general a 36-inch loom will serve you well and the difference in price between the narrower ones and this size is surprisingly small. Remember, once you buy a narrow loom, you are limited for you cannot weave any wider than the width of your harnesses except by a technique of double width weaving which is usually considered more tedious than it is worth. On the other hand, it often happens that the wide loom is seldom used to its full capacity, and all it does is take up space.

Another item to be considered is the placement of the treadles on the framework of the loom. Notice that those on the loom illustrated are bolted to the front or heel bar of the loom. On a four-harness loom of this style this makes the treadling very easy because the weaver can slide the foot along the treadle towards the rear of it to obtain good leverage. When the treadles are fastened at the rear of the loom so that the front ends are free, they often wobble from side to side, making them more difficult to find with the feet. For this reason, my own preference is for treadles which are fastened at the front of the loom.

Beaters on a loom may be of two styles also. Some are like the one mentioned, fastened at the side of the loom near the floor. Others are known as *overhead* or *hanging beaters* and are fastened from a rocking shaft at the top of the loom. I do not enjoy weaving on a loom of this sort, myself, but am told that for the weaving of tweeds and woolens it is especially desirable. The looms manufactured in Norway, Sweden, and Denmark are usually of this kind.

But the most important decision you will have to make with regard to your loom, aside from the cost, make, and size of it, will be the matter of whether you are going to have what is called a *sinking shed* loom like the one we have been describing thus far or a *rising shed* loom.

To try to explain the difference between them before you (presumably) know anything about weaving is like trying to put the cart before the horse. However, the *sinking shed loom* has its harnesses suspended from the top of the loom in such a way that when they are fastened to the lamms beneath them and the lamms to the treadles beneath *them,* the harnesses operate in pairs. As we have already found out this was brought about by the use of three rollers and cords. Some looms like this have other means of hanging the harnesses, but they are not as satisfactory. (See page 111.) The sinking shed loom is also called the *counterbalanced loom,* because when it is in operation, the weaver steps on certain of the treadles and in so doing pulls down two of the harnesses *while at the same time the other two rise.* In other words, the harnesses are counterbalanced two against two. Many, perhaps most, of the modern looms in use today are of this type and so were the huge old looms made of hand-hewn logs upon which the old Colonial coverlets were woven on four harnesses.

The *rising shed loom,* on the other hand, operates on quite a different principle. There are no rollers with their cords or any of the other methods of suspension of harnesses referred to in connection with the sinking shed loom. The usual type of rising shed loom is equipped with levers called *jacks* and so is often referred to as a *jack type loom.* Jacks are levers which may be found above or below the harnesses and which pivot at or near the middle. When one end of the levers is pulled down by means of a cord going from the lever to a lamm, the other end lifts or pushes up the harness but, unlike the action of the sinking shed loom, the other harnesses do not move. Not all rising shed looms operate by means of jacks, for there are also roller lamms which, when used in connection with cords and pulleys, act somewhat on the principle of a window sash. Because the harnesses of a rising shed loom are not counterbalanced, they do not need to operate in pairs but can be used one at a time, two at a time and three at a time with no difficulty. The advantage of the rising shed lies in this fact, for there are many instances when it is not only desirable but necessary for harnesses to do this. The loom with counterbalanced harnesses and sinking shed does not, as a general rule, take kindly to such treatment. (See however page 143.)

If I were starting out all over again to buy my equipment for weaving, I would think seriously about the rising shed floor loom for the reason given above. Of course, there are many arguments in favor of the sinking shed loom. They are less noisy to operate and less expensive to buy. The noise of harnesses returning to their resting position can be quite an item if you do not have a loom room away from the rest of the household. Finally, most directions for treadling a loom are given for the counterbalanced loom so that it becomes necessary to transpose them for the rising shed. This is not a valid objection, however, for once you start weaving and observe what happens as a loom operates, the change of treadling from one type loom to the other becomes easy. Directions are given for transposing in Chapters 9 and 10.

It is true that there is more strain put upon the warp threads when a loom has the rising shed, and this is largely the reason why weavers are not in agreement on the subject of which type is better.

The question of what kind of warp beam to have on your loom can be settled easily, for you can have both what is known as a *sectional beam* and a *plain beam* inasmuch as they are generally interchangeable. Also the expense of the extra beam is not great. Further discussion of plain beams and sectional beams and what the difference is, is left for Chapters 4 and 10. The loom pictured has a plain beam. Warp beams which hold spools of warp are not usually found as standard equipment on floor looms. A discussion of ready-spooled warp will be found on page 21, and the novice will find out in the next chapter what the word *warp* is all about.

Thus far we have mentioned only floor looms, but there are also on the market table looms either with or without stands. Of the rising shed type, the harnesses of table looms are operated not by the feet (unless treadles are purchased separately), but by the use of hand levers. Four-harness table looms are narrower than most floor looms so they take up much less space, and many of them are easily carried from one place to another. They are handy to have as accessory looms and for teaching purposes though their price, unfortunately, is not proportionate to their size. The exhilaration which comes when both the hand and the feet are used in rhythmic weaving, however, can only be experienced from the use of a floor loom.

Both table looms and floor looms may be had in the folding models, and folding table looms are particularly convenient to take to guild meetings and weaving conferences. Folding floor looms are somewhat more expensive than the rigid type and some are likely to be less firm. However, there are excellent folding looms available.

The equipment a weaver requires does not end with the acquisition of a loom and shuttles. It is wise, for instance, to buy the bench recommended by the manufacturer so that it will be suitable to the height of the breast beam from the floor. Other pieces of equipment are necessary as aids in the preparation of a loom for weaving and for the weaving itself. It is the purpose of the first part of *A Handweaver's Workbook* to acquaint you with these and to instruct in their use.

Chapter references: "What Loom Shall I Buy?" by Bill Carter. *Handweaver & Craftsman,* Vol. 3 No. 4 and Vol. 5 No. 1. "If You Plan to Buy a Loom." Bulletin of the Shuttle Craft Guild.

Chapter 2

GETTING READY

As your loom comes from the manufacturer, not very often is it ready for you to use. It is up to you, therefore, to go through certain preliminaries known as the *setting-up process*.

SELECTING THE WARP

Part of this preparation consists of the selection of the warp you are going to use. This warp yarn or thread will then be made into a set of parallel strands called *warp ends* which are to be stretched lengthwise on your loom before any weaving can begin. Inasmuch as cloth is woven not only of these lengthwise threads but also of crosswise threads, you will need in addition what is known as *weft*. *Woof* as a synonym for weft is now becoming obsolete although it is a term still used by many of the older weavers. The commercial term *filling* is also sometimes used by handweavers to mean the crosswise threads or weft.

The thread chosen for warp must be strong and suitable for the fabric desired. For rag rugs, for instance, a thread called carpet warp is often used and this can be bought at most five-and-ten-cent stores. For luncheon sets, runners, table cloths, some bag and dress materials, a cotton warp known as 20/2 ("twenties-two," or in Canada "two-twenties") might be your choice. For linen towels, table linens, and linen dress materials a suitable warp would be a 40/2 (forties-two) linen. There are many sources of weaving supplies. You will find their advertisements in the periodicals mentioned in the bibliography, and you should send for their catalogs and sample cards.

Suppose we decide to use some of this finer 20/2 warp in the natural color. This is a warp which does not offer too many problems for the novice, yet is a little more intricate than plain carpet warp would be. With this 20/2 cotton warp we shall go through all the operations necessary to put the warp on the loom, to thread it to a pattern and then to weave it.

ALLOWING FOR DRAW-IN

A good width to plan to weave at first is 14 inches, which means 14 inches for the material when woven. In order that the fabric will be 14 inches wide when off the loom, it is necessary to plan so that the width of the warp on the loom will be greater. The necessity for this is something referred to by weavers as *draw-in*. No matter how excellent a weaver a person is, the finished material is never as wide as the warp on the loom even before it is laundered. This draw-in or shrinkage in width varies not only according to the type of warp yarn used but also with the weft. Moreover, some weavers just naturally seem to draw in more than others when they weave. There are other things, too, about which we will speak later in Chapter 10 that cause drawing in. Much of the time a weaver must lean upon past experience for a guide. Therefore, for this narrow warp it is sufficient to say now that we will prepare the warp to be 15 inches wide on the loom, or one inch wider than we wish the material to be. This will take care of the draw-in of even a beginner.

A 20/2 cotton warp woven into fabric is usually found to have thirty warp ends in each inch of its width. Carpet warp is much heavier than 20/2 and so is planned for fewer warp ends per inch. For instance, if rag rugs are to be woven, then not more than twelve warp ends should be in each inch across the rug. Of course, the more warp ends there are per inch the finer the material is. Some warps are made very much finer than this, but the usual number is thirty for 20/2.

FIGURING THE NUMBER OF WARP ENDS

Now we can begin to plan the warp we are going to put on the loom. It is to be fifteen inches wide, and in each inch there will be thirty warp ends. Multiplying fifteen by thirty we have as a result 450 warp ends across the warp. If you examine any piece of yard goods you will see at the right and left side of it a narrow strip where the threads are closer together. This is called a *selvage*. In order to allow for the narrowing in at the selvages, we add at least four warp ends at each side of every piece of weaving. If we did not allow these extra warp ends at the sides, the beginning and end of the pattern which we are going to thread later on would be distorted by the aforementioned draw-in. Even if we do not weave in a pattern but just make plain material, we still add for the selvages in order to improve the appearance and wearing qualities of the weaving. What to do with the selvages and how to thread a pattern is discussed in another chapter.

The warp we are going to put on the loom, therefore, will have 458 warp ends in it, or thirty for each inch of width plus eight for the selvages. The exact number of thirty per inch will be maintained during the weaving by the use of the reed (E). In this instance, we will use a reed that has sixteen steel partitions per inch. The spaces between are called *dents*, so this is known as a 15-dent reed. In each dent we will put two warp ends. A carpet warp prepared so as to have twelve warp ends for each inch of the material's width would require the use of a 12-dent reed and one warp end would be put through each dent. Or, a 6-dent reed could be used and two warp ends put through each of the dents. It is the reed, therefore, that keeps the weaving at the width desired, and its dentage and number of warp ends per dent determine the fineness or coarseness of the material. All this is anticipating a bit, for the reed is not used right now.

Reeds of all different sizes and lengths may be purchased from supply houses. Be sure to specify how long a reed you want and how many dents per inch are needed. Most looms are furnished with 15-dent reeds, but you will need others as the scope of your weaving widens.

SPOOLED WARP

Many table looms and a few floor looms are equipped with hexagonal steel beams about ½ inch in diameter. These are for use with what are called *ready warped spools*. If you have one of these looms, buy one spool of warp for each two-inch width of the material you plan to weave. Spooled warp may be purchased from most supply houses. Because your warp is already wound for you if you have this type of loom, you will not need to go through the processes to be described in the next three chapters. You will, however, have to know how to thread a pattern, so read Chapter 6 carefully.

Chapter reference: *The Arithmetic of Weaving.* One of many "Practical Weaving Suggestions" prepared by the Lily Mills Company, Shelby, North Carolina. $1.00 annual subscription. Send for their samples and price list, also.

Chapter 3

PREPARING THE WARP FOR A LOOM WITH A PLAIN BEAM

The following directions are for the preparation of a warp for a loom that has what is called a "plain beam." If your loom has a warp beam which is studded with wooden or metal pegs that divide its length into small sections, skip this part and refer to the next chapter, where you will find ·instructions for the sectional beam.

There are two pieces of equipment, either of which may be used for the preparation of a warp on this type of beam. First, let us consider the one called the *warping frame.* The alternate method is the use of a *warping reel,* and a description of it and its use will be found later in this chapter.

THE WARPING FRAME AND ITS USE

Warping frames may be purchased or made at home. The one which my classes use was made by a carpenter and is permanently fixed to the wall. It is larger than the usual ones, being made of one-inch pine with one-inch dowels, ten inches long, which are spaced far enough apart in the frame so that the knuckles do not get bumped when the warp is being prepared on it. (See Illustration 3.) Usually these frames have the distance between peg A and peg D equal a yard instead of two yards as here. The distance between peg A and B is 18 inches and between peg B and peg C seven inches, but any other suitable dimensions could have been used. A drill press was used to bore the holes in order that the

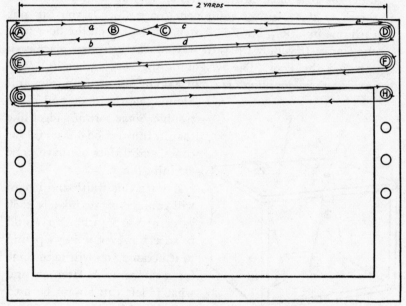

Illustration 3. Warping frame.

dowels which fit tightly in them might be absolutely perpendicular. If they are not, the dowels, not being at right angles to the frame, will cause the last threads wound on them to be shorter (or maybe longer) than the first ones and this will make the warp a troublesome one to handle.

Apparently, however, this item did not worry some of the early weavers very much, for down in the Southern Appalachian Highlands I have seen warping frames leaning against the outside walls of the mountain cabins ready for use. The pegs were made of corn cobs!

The following is a step-by-step description of the method of preparing a warp prior to putting it on the warp beam. When finished, you will have 458 warp ends lying side by side, each ten yards long.

1. Place two spools or tubes of the 20/2 cotton warp (of course any other warp is handled in this same way) on a spool rack. See sketch of this piece of equipment (page 43). Or you can put each one in a deep bowl or wastepaper basket on the floor near the frame. If your warp yarn was bought in cones, place each cone on the floor. The weight of the cones when full will prevent them toppling over, but as they are used up, they roll around on the floor and cause trouble. Some sort of gadget like that in Illustration 4 is useful for cones, and it does not have to be anything fancy.

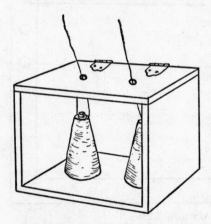

A warp this width and length will contain approximately 4580 yards of warp yarn. You would be wise, however, to buy a pound of it because you will need some for weaving with later on and what is left can always be used for other things. There are 8400 yards in a pound of 20/2 warp. Purchase it in two half pounds so as to save yourself the bother of winding part of it on to a spool in order to have two warp ends.

Illustration 4. A handy arrangement for holding cones of warp yarn for use with either a warping frame or warping reel. Two small dowels fastened into the bottom of the box hold the cones in place.

Or, if the manufacturer does not sell it in half pounds, you can buy it in two-ounce tubes.

If the warp is in skeins, it must be wound into balls or on to large spools. To hold the skeins while this is being done, you will find a skein holder, known also as a *swift,* very convenient. When winding yarn into balls, begin by wrapping it around a small stone or other weight. This will prevent balls of yarn from bouncing around when you are using them. Two spools, balls, cones, etc., are needed because, to save time, two warp ends are going to be wound on at the same time. While it is true that some weavers wind on four warp ends at a time, it has always been my sad experience that more time is spent later on untangling the warp ends during the weaving than it is worth. Therefore, I never wind any more than two at once of any fiber when preparing a warp this way. On the other hand, it is usually considered a waste of time to wind on only one end at a time.

2. Take the two ends coming from your spools, etc., tie them together, then tie them around peg A of the warping frame. Follow Illustration 3 as you read what follows:

3. Let the two ends run easily through your fingers as you draw them from the spools and separate them by keeping the first finger of your guiding hand between them at all times.

4. Bring these two ends *over* peg B and *under* peg C. Then over and under each of pegs D, E, F, G, and H, which in this instance is the end peg because you are winding ten yards for this, your first, warp. Do not use much tension as you wind, but keep it uniform throughout. Too much tension will cause the pegs to lean inward and may even snap them off. This once happened when one of my students was winding with a little too much enthusiasm. When you have reached peg H, you have wound on this frame two warp ends, each ten yards long.

5. Now start to wind back up to peg A. Do this by bringing the warp ends from peg H across to peg G. *Under* G and over on top of it and so across to F. Under F, up and over to E and continue in this manner *under* pegs E and D.

6. But now go *over* peg C and *under* peg B (just the opposite from that which you did on the way down) and from B straight across and *under* peg A ready to start again.

7. Repeat steps 4, 5, and 6 over and over again. You will notice
that on the way down from A to H you carry the warp ends
over the pegs D, E, F, G, and H, while on the way up from
H to A you place them *under* these same pegs. As you wind up
and down the frame, take care to place each two warp ends
alongside of the last ones on each peg and do not allow them
to pile up one on top of the other. When, however, the pegs
begin to get filled up push the strands of warp already wound
down toward the base of each peg so they will not slip off. If
they should tend to fall off at the ends of the pegs in spite of
this, a rubber band wound around each peg at its outer end will
be of great help.

8. As the winding progresses it is necessary to count the number of
warp ends wound. This counting is done between pegs B and C
where the warp ends cross. I find it easy to count by fifties, so
when I have wound twenty-five of the double strands I tie these
fifty warp ends off with a piece of colored carpet warp between
pegs B and C, leaving the ends of my tying thread long enough
to tie off the next fifty and so on for the entire 458 desired. Do
not use a hard knot here for these ties are only temporary ones.

NOTE: The cross which you can see is being formed between pegs B and
        C is absolutely necessary and must be correctly made. Its object
        is to keep the warp ends in order, two by two, as they are wound.
        The necessity for this will become apparent when certain steps
        in the setting-up process are made later on.

9. When a knot appears in the warp yarn as you are winding,
it is best to eliminate it immediately rather than let it stay in
and be put on the loom. Suppose there is a knot in the warp
coming from one of the spools when you are halfway between
peg D and E, for instance. Break off the warp end which has
the knot in it *back at peg A* (the nearest end peg). Break the
same warp end at the knot discarding the thread in between
the end peg and that point. Now tie the end coming from the
spool onto the end at peg A and go on winding as before.

Knots that occur or are made at or near the end pegs A and H, that is, the beginning and end pegs, will not come into the woven portion of the warp so they do not matter. Any others should be eliminated as described above even though this may mean cutting off several yards of warp.

The same process takes care of a spool of warp which runs out before the others. Tie the new one on at either the beginning or the end peg, whichever is the nearer.

Also, the same procedure is followed in the case of a striped warp. To wind a warp in inch-wide stripes of alternating blue and natural 20/2, for instance, take two spools of the blue and two of the natural and put them on your spool rack. Wind thirty ends of the blue (this would be fifteen double strands at the cross). Then break off the blue ends, and tie on to them the two ends coming from the natural colored spools. In this instance the tying will take place at peg H. Wind on another thirty ends. Cut the natural colored warp ends off, this time at peg A, and attach the two blue again. It is not necessary to tie each blue to each natural. Simply take the two of one color and tie them to the two of the other. The reason for winding thirty ends of each color to make one-inch stripes is because we planned to use thirty ends per inch, you will remember. For a heavier warp, such as carpet warp, twelve or fifteen warp ends would be sufficient for each stripe, depending upon the number of dents in each inch of your reed.

10. When the winding is completed, you will have nine bunches of warp ends tied up with colored ties. The last bunch will have 58 warp ends in it, making 458 in all. Remember, these are 458 single warp ends or 229 double strands, meaning that you will have gone down and up the frame 229 times in all.

11. To end, take the two warp ends coming from the spools, tie them around the nearest end peg, and cut them off. The next step must be done very carefully. Tie the warp strands securely at the four places marked on the illustration as a, b, c, and d. These ties hold in place the crosses formed between pegs B and

C. Make these ties with a colored carpet warp drawn tightly, and use a bowknot (like tying a shoelace) which can be pulled out easily later on without any need for scissors.

12. Now pull out the colored tie which you used to count the warp ends. This is no longer needed.

NOTE: It can be seen that warp wound like this, two ends at a time, results in an even number of warp ends. If at any time it is necessary or desirable for you to use a pattern that needs an odd number of warp ends, wind an even number, and the extra warp end can be used to make one of the selvages wider when threading the pattern.

13. The warp must be removed from the frame, of course, but you will find that it helps to tie it in several more places first, as follows: Make one tight tie about four feet from the cross over towards peg D. This is marked *e* on the sketch and is called the *brake* or *choker tie* because it prevents snarls and tangles from going farther down the length of the warp while it is being spread either through the reed or what is called a raddle as described in Chapter 5. Also tie the warp halfway between pegs D and E, E and F, F and G, etc., or, if your frame is smaller than this one, at points corresponding to every yard of the warp. Finally, tie the warp where it turns around pegs A and H. Take care here to catch the very first and last loops you tied on these pegs. All these ties should be tight and fastened with bowknots so that they can be pulled out later.

14. The warp is now ready for you to remove it from the frame by a process called *chaining the warp*. If you are familiar with the art of crocheting, this will be simple for it is the same thing, using the hands instead of a hook. First, however, remove your wrist watch and all jewelry which might catch in the warp ends. Buttons, especially on cuffs, can be a terrible nuisance.

Begin at peg H and take the thick strand of warp off this peg holding the entire warp taut as you do so to prevent it from slipping off the other pegs. From below put your right hand into the loop where peg H was and grasp the entire warp strand (marked *c* on Illustration 5) with this same hand. Draw your handful of warp through the loop around your wrist, and as you do this, the loop will slip forward and off the back of your right hand. Keep hold of the warp in your right hand and then put your left hand into the loop which you are holding. Reach through this loop to grasp the warp coming from the peg at *c* and pull it back through the loop, thus making a chain. Let go of the warp in the right hand, but keep on holding the loop which you have in your left. Now insert

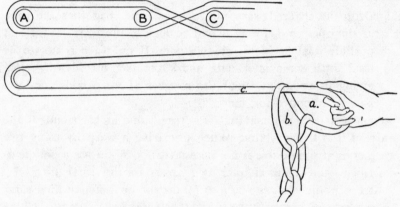

Illustration 5. Chaining off the warp.

the right hand into the loop being held by the left hand, grasp the strand of warp and bring it through, thus forming another chain. The chains may be tight or loose as you prefer. Continue alternating with right and left hands until the brake tie (e, Illustration 3) is reached. At this point, tie a piece of colored thread around the chain of warp so that it cannot ravel out. The sketch of this process of chaining the warp shows that this all sounds much more complicated than it actually is for it is nothing but a simple chain stitch done with the hands.

Some weavers prefer to use one hand to make the chain rather than alternating hands. This is satisfactory, too. Just be sure in either case that your hand goes through the loop marked *a* on the sketch and not through *b* for if it goes through *b* the chain will be locked and will not unwind from that point on. The chaining of the warp is but a temporary process and it is necessary to unchain it later.

NOTE: Someday you may want to wind a wide warp 36 inches wide, for instance. You will have better results if you wind it in two parts— half the width and chain it off; the other half and chain off. Later slip the two sections on to the lease sticks together and treat them as one warp.

15. Drop the chained warp into a large paper bag with the cross at the open end, for it is best to handle the warp as little as possible until it is put on the loom. If the warp is not to be used until some later date, mark the bag for identification, giving information about the number of warp ends, yardage, pattern intended for, etc.

Some texts suggest making two crosses, one at each end of the warp as it is being wound. When preparing a warp by using two warp ends at a time this is not necessary, but if you use a paddle as described later in this chapter, two crosses are the usual thing.

At this point you are ready to follow the next steps which carry on the process known as *dressing the loom*. See, therefore, Chapter 5.

THE WARPING REEL AND ITS USE

In place of a warping frame, any warp for a plain beam may be prepared with the use of a warping reel. A *warping reel* (see Illustration 6) may be bought from loom manufacturers or supply houses. Each turn of the reel winds on two or more yards of warp depending upon the circumference of the reel. The boards marked 1 and 2 on the sketch and which hold the lower and upper pegs may be moved up or down the reel so that warps of various lengths may be wound on it. The warping reel is very easy to use once you get into the swing of it and is also less tiring than the other method. Here is the way it is done:

1. Determine where to place the adjustable board (1) which holds

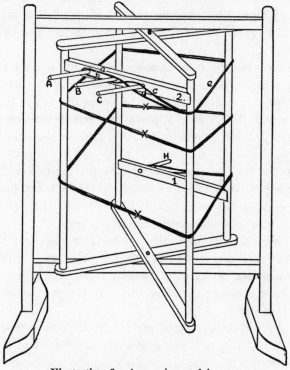

Illustration 6. A warping reel in use.

the end peg H. This is done by tying to peg A a measured length of thread which differs in color from your warp yarn. Spin the reel clockwise, and when the end of this strand is reached, there place board 1, tying the end of the colored thread to peg H. However, because board 1 and board 2 are on opposite sides of the reel in order to balance the weight of it, it may not be possible to wind exactly the amount you had planned. For instance, instead of ten yards, on a reel with a three-yard circumference, you will have to wind ten and one-half yards. This will be three turns of the wheel plus the yard and a half to get back to the end board.

Space the spirals made by the colored thread as evenly as possible on the framework of the reel and mark them with masking tape. This experimental warp end is left on the reel as a ready guide but is discarded when the warp is chained off the reel.

2. Place your two tubes or spools of warp on a spool rack (also called a creel), or in a deep bowl just as in the first method. Take the two ends and tie them around the peg at the bottom of the reel (H). You can place this board with its end peg at the top if you prefer to have the cross at the bottom of the reel.

3. Rotate the reel counterclockwise, keeping the two ends of warp separated by your index finger. As the reel turns, guide these warp ends so that they lay directly next to the colored warp thread, all the way up to the top of the reel.

4. The board (2) has in it three dowels or pegs and these correspond to those around which the cross was made on the warping frame. Refer to the sketch of the reel, and guide your warp ends *over* peg C, *under* peg B and then straight across to the left of peg A.

5. Give the reel another spin and carry the two warp ends over peg A across to peg B going *over* B and *under* peg C (just the opposite from the way it was done on the way up) and thence alongside of the first spirals and up and down the reel until the required 458 warp ends are wound. This means 229 times for we are winding on two ends at a time. Do not let the bands of warp get too wide; after every few turns of the reel push them into as narrow a width as possible.

6. Count off the warp ends by fifties (25 strands of two each), as in the warping frame method. When the warp is wound, you will have eight groups of 50 counted and tied plus the last one of 58.

7. Then tie the cross at a, b, c, d using colored thread, making

the ties snug and using bowknots pulled tight. About four feet
from peg C at the place indicated as *e*, make another very snug
tie. This is the *choker* or *brake tie* and it will prevent snarls
from going down the length of the warp later on. Make ties
around the bands of warp at the places indicated by an x mark.
The warp is also tied at the beginning and end pegs taking
care to catch the first and last loops which were tied around
them. Use colored thread for all these ties, make them snug
and use bowknots, such as are used when tying your shoes.

8. Chain off the warp just as was done in the warping frame
method. Most warping reels are vertical, like the one shown,
so you will have to be careful not to relax the tension of the
warp while chaining it or the whole thing will fall down
towards the floor and become wound around the place where
the reel rotates at the bottom. To prevent this, I stand on one
foot while holding the reel from turning too rapidly with the
other. Perhaps you can make some sort of a brake for your
reel which will eliminate the need for these gymnastics. Reels
which are horizontal are available, and I find them much more
easy to operate.

Some weavers, having gained experience, find it satisfactory to
put a warp directly from a horizontal reel on to the warp beam of
the loom without chaining it off first. In this event, a brake is
necessary or the assistance of another person to put tension on the
reel while the warp is being put on the beam. Except for the
elimination of the chaining process, the method of putting a warp
on a loom directly from the reel is practically the same as described
in the next chapters. It works well, however, only if the warp has
been prepared on the reel with uniform tension so a novice would
do well to follow the standard procedures.

PREPARING A WARP WITH THE USE OF A PADDLE

After you have acquired skill in the preparation of a warp by
either of the methods just given, try making one with the use of
what is known as a *paddle*. I suggest you do this only after you have

gained some experience, for the handling of many warp ends at a time in the paddle can be infuriating if they catch on shoelaces, trouser cuffs, skirt hems, buttons, and other nearby things. But there is nothing about this method which you cannot master once confidence has been won. With a paddle a number of warp ends can be wound on at a time though sixteen is usually considered the upper limit.

Paddles may be purchased but are easily made of soft wood one-quarter or a half-inch thick. Fashion the wood into a rectangular piece about two inches wide by six inches long and sand it very smooth. The paddle may be made with a handle like that of a hand mirror if desired. Bore holes into the paddle in two vertical rows as shown in Illustration 7. You will also need a creel or spool rack like that shown in the chapter on Sectional Beaming.

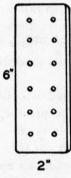

6″

2″

Illustration 7. A paddle used for preparing a warp. This one can accommodate twelve warp ends.

Let us for demonstration purposes prepare a warp of 458 ends with the paddle, winding it six warp ends at a time on the warping frame (though a reel could just as well be used). Make this a striped warp—two blue warp ends followed by four white ones. The reason for putting stripes in your first warp done this way will be explained presently. Proceed as follows:

1. Place four spools of white warp and two spools of blue on the creel in two vertical rows side by side with the two blue warp spools at the bottom, one in each row. Twenties-two warp may be bought on small tubes of 1050 yards each, but if you do not wish to go to this expense, you must wind off your warp on to six spools. Each spool must, of course, have sufficient warp wound on it to complete the entire warp. For a ten-yard warp put on 500 yards per spool which is more than the exact amount

needed but better than not enough. A yarn measurer, such as the one mentioned in the next chapter, is a useful accessory to have for keeping count of the yardage put on the spools.

2. See that the warp thread winds off the spools from the same direction, either from underneath them or from the top of them.

3. Thread the ends from the spools one at a time through the holes of the paddle, putting each warp end into that hole of the paddle which corresponds to its place and row on the creel. Tie these ends to peg A of the warping frame.

4. Put elastic bands around the free ends of pegs A, B, C, and H to help prevent the warp ends from falling off them as the winding progresses.

Making the Cross

The cross, which you remember occurs between pegs B and C, is now going to be made on your fingers with the help of the paddle and then transferred from your fingers to these pegs in a process something like making a "cat's cradle" with string.

1. Stand with your back to the warping board and draw the paddle towards you along the six warp ends. Hold the paddle so that the two blue warp ends are at the bottom of it just as they are on the creel.

2. Hold the paddle with your left hand at the same time grasping all the warp ends coming from the paddle on the creel side as shown in Illustration 8. This puts a tension on the warp ends coming from the board.

3. As you face the paddle, note that the six warp ends are in two vertical rows coming from the holes of the paddle. There is a row composed of three warp ends in front (that is, towards you) and another row of three towards the rear or away from you. (The sketch shows a paddle carrying ten warp ends.) The lowest warp end in each row is a blue one.

4. Still keeping your body between the warping frame and the

paddle, place the ball of your right index finger *on top of* that
warp end which is at the bottom of the row near you. It is a blue
warp end. Reach *under* this same warp end with your right
thumb, and then place the ball of the thumb on top of the warp
end which is coming from the lowest hole of the back row of the
paddle. It, too, is blue. Now you have crossed these two warp
ends as shown in the sketch. Push them down on your thumb
and index finger towards the knuckles ready for the next two.

5. Reach up with your same index finger and place the ball of
   it on top of the second lowest warp end on the front row
   (white). Your thumb then goes under this warp end and over
   the second lowest one in the other row (also white) to complete
   the crossing of two more warp ends. Push these back also
   towards your knuckles.

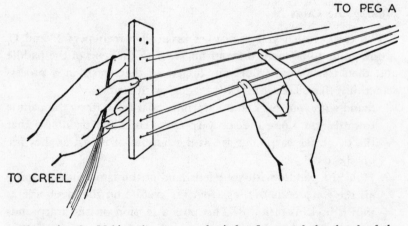

TO PEG A

TO CREEL

Illustration 8. Making the cross on the index finger and the thumb of the
right hand. Pegs B and C, not shown, would be to the right of the sketch. Direction shown is that of winding from peg A to the end peg.

6. Repeat the same operation with the other two warp ends. Now
   all six warp ends have been crossed. Transfer them directly
   from your thumb and index finger to pegs B and C. Those from
   the index finger go on peg B; those from the thumb to peg
   C. This results in a single cross . . . that is, a cross composed

of single warp ends alternating over and under these two pegs. The blue warp ends are the first two of the warp. Push the warp ends well down the pegs.

7. Still holding the paddle in your left hand, slide it down the warp ends to a place near your waist as you take all six of them in your right hand and wind them on the pegs of the warping frame just as was done in the two-thread method, until peg H is reached.

The Portee Cross

When using this method to prepare a warp it is usual to make at the end of the warp a second cross called the *portee cross* to distinguish it from the first one which is known as the *porrey cross*. It is at the portee cross that the warp ends are most easily counted. Make the portee cross as follows:

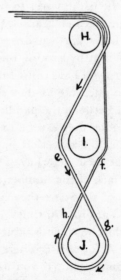

1. Bring all six warp ends to the top of peg H as usual then make a six warp end turn around pegs I and J and back again to peg H as shown in Illustration 9. The paddle is not used at all in making this cross but remains in your left hand out of the way. Warping boards commercially made have pegs providing for the making of this second cross, but the sketch shows how the vertical pegs along the side of a warping board may be used for the purpose.

2. Bring the paddle up to peg H then turn the paddle so

Illustration 9. The portee cross as made on vertical pegs I and J of the warping board. Letters e, f, g, and h indicate where the cross is to be tied.

that the two blue threads which were on the bottom of it when winding down the board are now on top. It was for this reason that two colors of warp were recommended for this demonstration. Whether the warp is to be a striped one or all one color, the paddle is nevertheless turned end for end.

3. Push the paddle along with the left hand winding on the warp for the return trip until peg C is reached.

4. Here the paddle is used again to make the cross on the fingers with this difference: this time face the warping board. Keep the paddle in the left hand and use the right hand to cross the warp ends starting at the bottom as before. The first cross made will, due to the turning of the paddle, be made with two white warp ends. When all six have been crossed transfer them to pegs B and C. The warp ends on the thumb go on peg B, those on the index finger are slipped on peg C and all are pushed well back on these pegs.

5. Bring the paddle over to peg A and as you do so turn it so that the blue warp ends are again the two at the bottom of the rows of the holes, and you are ready to start all over again. Now you can see that by turning the paddle at the beginning and end of the warp you have caused the blue and the white stripes of warp ends to alternate as they should. If the warp ends become too twisted between the paddle and the creel due to this turning of the paddle, they can be untwisted at either peg A or peg H by reversing the direction in which the paddle is turned. Twists made at these pegs have no effect on the warp's preparation.

6. Keep track of the number of warp ends wound by counting the groups of six where they cross between pegs I and J. When you have 76 groups (76 times 6 equals 456 warp ends) break off the four white warp ends. Pull them out of the paddle and tie them to peg A for this is where the winding of 76 groups will have been completed. (If you had been winding an uneven number of these groups of six, 77 for example, then this would occur at peg J, which actually is the end peg.) Wind the four slack ends of white back on to their respective spools on the creel.

7. Make a cross with the remaining two blue warp ends and slip them on pegs B and C. Then, having wound them on the other pegs and made the portee cross with them, fasten them off and tie them to peg J. This completes 458 warp ends and assures that the warp will be balanced with a blue stripe at beginning and end.

8. Tie the porrey cross (the one at pegs B and C) in four places as usual.

9. Tie the portee cross in four places where marked on the sketch as e, f, g, and h.

10. Make any other ties as is your custom.

11. *Beginning at peg A,* chain off the warp from the board, leaving it unchained from peg H to J.

Reason for Change of Position

You, no doubt, wonder why the first cross is made while standing with your back to the warping board when winding down the board and while facing it on the way up. It is done so that the right hand may be used. If you stand facing the board when about to make the cross with your fingers and peg A is at your left, the paddle must be held in the right hand and the left hand used for crossing the warp ends . . . an awkward process for a right-handed person.

It was also done to keep the alternation of the warp ends exact. Try doing it while facing the board both on the downward and the return trip and you will see that there is always one place where two warp ends do not alternate on pegs B and C, even though the paddle is turned end for end. This, however, is not really objectionable inasmuch as they could be separated later on when selecting them for threading.

PROS AND CONS

Obviously preparing a warp by using more than two warp ends at a time has its advantages. Those who do not like the method, however, say that they can use two warp ends at once much more rapidly than they can stop to make the cross each time plus the fact that there is no need then to wind warp off on to many spools. Here again, of course, is a matter of personal opinion. Many experienced weavers, especially those who learned the craft years ago, make the cross on their fingers with a rhythm and speed that is a delight to see.

By one method or the other you have prepared a warp which is to be placed on a loom with a plain beam. Further instructions will be found in Chapter 5.

One more thing. Try to finish the preparation of a warp all at one time. If you leave the task and return to it later, there will be a change in the tension with which you hold the warp ends. This causes slack spots to occur in the warp, and these are troublesome when it is being wound on the warp beam of your loom. Indeed, "Finish your warping before night, or sit up nights with your weaving," is a warning which it is well worth while to heed.

Chapter 4

WINDING A WARP ON A SECTIONAL BEAM

If your loom has a sectional beam, you will find that the beam at the rear is divided into small sections, usually two inches wide, by means of wooden or metal pegs. Or you may have a sectional beam as an added feature of your loom, interchangeable with or additional to the plain beam. Each section of this type of beam must be wound separately for the full length of the warp desired. This does away with the need for either a warping frame or a warping reel.

In order to wind the warp on the two-inch sections evenly, you must have a *tensioner,* also called a *tension box*. It is necessary also to wind off your warp yarn on to many spools or to buy it on small (usually two-ounce) tubes.

To be consistent, plan to wind on to the sectional beam the same width and length as was mentioned in Chapter 2, namely, ten yards, 15 inches wide. Use as before a 20/2 cotton yarn in natural color for the warp. Ordinarily, it is wise to try to have the total number of warp ends you are going to wind exactly divisible into the two-inch sections of the warp beam. Usually a 20/2 warp yarn is planned for thirty ends per inch so in each two-inch section of this beam there would be sixty warp ends. To wind each section, therefore, would require sixty spools or tubes of warp yarn, each spool containing enough warp yarn to wind the ten yards planned for in each and every section.

The trouble is that the 458 warp ends decided upon in Chapter 2 is not a figure exactly divisible by sixty. If you wind seven of the sections with each one containing sixty ends, you will have only 420 ends. If you wind eight sections, you have too many warp ends. Do not wind seven sections with 60 warp ends in each and then wind one more section with only 38 ends in it for the tension of this last section will never match the others. What, then, to do?

There is no objection to having the warp on the warp beam spread out a little wider than the fifteen inches planned for in the reed. In fact, it is a very good thing for there is then less friction on the selvage threads in the reed. Therefore, your solution is to place upon the spool rack fifty-eight spools of warp and by following the directions given wind any two of the sections with 58 warp ends and six with 57, making 458 in all.

You can also, if you prefer, wind eight sections with sixty warp ends each and then later on when you are threading them discard 22 warp ends of the last section. But this is wasteful and the 22 unused warp ends wind around the warp beam, make a nuisance of themselves and have to be cut off from time to time.

Here, then, is the way a sectional beam is wound:

1. First measure the circumference of your warp beam, so you will know how many turns of the crank to make for the desired ten-yard length of warp. Perhaps the catalog for your loom will tell you this without having to measure the beam.

2. Place 58 spools or tubes of warp yarn on the spool rack (also called a *creel*) so that all the ends coming from them wind off from the same direction, either from above or from below. (See Illustration 10.) Place the creel some distance from the rear of the loom.

3. Begin with the lowest spool on the right hand side of the creel, and thread its end through the tensioner. Take the end from the spool above this one and do likewise. When you reach the top of the first row of spools, begin at the bottom of the next. Not all makes of tensioners are like the one shown in Illustration 11 so read the directions sent with yours carefully. On some of them it is necessary to carry the first warp end over the first dowel, under the next, over the third and under the fourth, reversing the process with the second warp end.

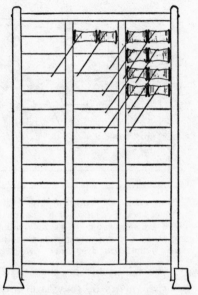

Illustration 10. A spool rack or creel. Full capacity of this model is 72 spools.

The tensioner shown, however, has removable dowels so that it is not necessary to do this. Each warp end as it is taken from the spool is put through a hole in a screen made of quarter-inch hardware cloth, beginning at the bottom of the screen at the left and entering the warp ends one by one in vertical rows. From there the warp ends are taken straight across under all the dowels and then put into the dents of a narrow reed which forms part of the tensioner. When all the warp ends are threaded through the hardware cloth and through the reed, the first and third dowels are taken out, put under the ribbon of warp and inserted into holes in the side of the tensioner, thus exerting the required tension on the warp ends.

One advantage of this type of tensioner is its swinging reed which permits you to place the warp ends in the reed of the tensioner one or two to a dent and then, by swinging the reed,

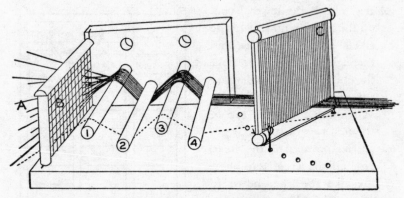

Illustration 11. Threading the tensioner. A. Warp ends coming from the creel or spool rack. B. Screen of hardware cloth. C. Swinging reed. Dowels marked 1 and 3 are removable. Extra holes above are for increasing the tension. Dotted line shows approximate position of the last warp end. (*Drawing based on tensioner manufactured by Loom Craft Studio, Wilmington, Ohio.*)

the width of the ribbon of warp strands can be adjusted to two inches or to whatever width is needed to fill the sections of your beam. If your tensioner does not have a swinging reed, arrange the warp ends in a 2-inch space in the reed which means, as a general thing, two in each dent.

Various arrangements are found for the securing of the tension box to a support during the winding on of the warp, but the most usual ones are made to clamp on the slabstock of the loom.

4. When all the warp ends have been put through the reed of the tensioner, tie them all to a long cord or narrow tape fastened to the center of the section you are preparing to wind. Each section must have one of these cords or tapes, all the same length and long enough to extend well up over the slabstock of the loom. They are usually provided with the loom, but if you make your own, use a slender cord doubled.

5. Not all warp beams are turned in the same direction. Some must be cranked clockwise and some counterclockwise. Don't make the mistake that I did once with a loom that was new to

me and wind on yards and yards of warp in the wrong direction! Watch for directional arrows on the warp beam or any directions given you with the loom. Lacking these, look carefully to see how the catch works on the ratchet of the warp beam and make sure that when the catch is on, the warp is not going to wind off the rear beam when you pull on it from the front of the loom.

Just how far back from the loom to place the creel is a matter for experimentation. Start at about eight feet and if the warp does not wind off the spools freely, increase the distance. Then keep the creel at this same distance all during the winding.

As the winding of each section is begun, it is important to see that the strand made up of the warp ends coming from the reed in the tensioner is centered in the section. Most important of all, watch that the warp ends do not pile up in the center of it or slough off at the sides or your tension will not be even. In other words, strive to keep the warp in each section as even as possible.

It is better to wind the center sections first, reserving the outer ones, where the selvages will be, for the last. They will be the better for the practice. Be sure, also, to center the warp on the beam, that is, use four sections on one side of the center and four on the other. If you had planned to use an uneven number of sections, this would not, of course, be possible but the warp should be centered as far as possible.

6. To keep track of the number of yards wound, you can count the turns of the crank. Let us hope there are no interruptions since it is all too easy to lose count. There are, however, different types of counters on the market which are attached to warp beams. There is also a very fine yardage counter available which takes the guesswork out of sectional beaming and is useful also when you are winding the spools or when you wish to know at any time how much of any yarn you have. I have found that this yardage counter soon pays for itself. If you do not have a

counter, better count the turns of the beam out loud and place on the warp beam a chalk mark to mark the place where each turn is to begin.

7. The strand or ribbon of warp coming from the tensioner winds on to each section with all warp ends lying side by side due to the reed provided with the tensioner. There is no way, however, of guaranteeing that the warp ends will stay in this order once they are cut. Therefore, to keep them side by side, when ten yards of warp have been wound on a section, take some masking or other gummed tape and lay it carefully under the strand of warp ends so that the threads are securely stuck to it *in order*. Then fold the tape over the top of the warp ends to make sure they will remain there.

8. Cut the ribbon of warp just beyond the gummed tape and toward the reed of the tensioner but hold all the ends coming from the reed so they do not snap back out of it. It is an excellent idea to tie them into a knot. Now pin the gummed tape to the section just wound. Mark with pencil on the tape a few cross marks so you will know the upper side of the strand of warp. Move the tensioner along, tie the warp strand to the next long cord, center the strand in the section, and wind on the same amount.

9. To wind those sections which are to have only 57 warp ends in them, simply remove one warp end from the tensioner and go on as before.

Directions for threading a warp put on sectionally are given in Chapter 6.

Chapter 5

SPREADING AND BEAMING THE WARP FOR A LOOM WITH A PLAIN BEAM

As has been seen, the use of a sectional beam accomplishes two operations at once: the preparation of the warp and the winding of it on to the warp beam. A warp for a plain beam, on the other hand, must first be prepared on a warping frame or warping reel as described in Chapter 3, after which it is wound on the warp beam. This is called *beaming,* and is one step of the entire procedure known as *dressing the loom,* or the setting-up process.

Fearing that they will get the warp hopelessly snarled, beginners approach this part of the setting-up process with a feeling of dread. Several things assure you, however, that your very first warp will go on easily. First of these was the choice you made in the fiber to be used, for cotton is not difficult for a learner to handle. You could have used wool of a well twisted type such as a worsted, but it is wise to avoid linen and rayon for warp until you have gained more experience. The newer man-made fibers (those known as *orlon, dacron,* etc.) can also be successfully handled by a

47

beginner, as a rule. The second factor which enters into the making of a good warp is the evenness of the tension at which the warp yarn was held during the winding on the frame or reel. Thirdly, care was taken to make a perfect cross, and when the warp was taken off the frame or reel, it was placed in a bag and handled as little as possible. You can, therefore, face your problem with confidence.

There is, really, no right or wrong way to beam a warp. Almost every writer on the subject and every weaver uses a little different method, and whichever you find is the easiest for you is the one to use. The method I prefer to use starts out by spreading the warp ends in the reed to the width desired and then goes on to wind it on to the warp beam as follows:

SPREADING THE WARP IN THE REED AT THE FRONT OF THE LOOM

This is a step which is preliminary to the beaming of the warp and by means of which it is spread out to the width desired, in this instance fifteen inches. If this were not done, the warp during the beaming would pile up on the warp beam whereas, for perfect weaving, it must wind on smoothly one warp end beside the other. The following steps accomplish this spreading:

1. Place the bag containing your chained warp on the floor in front of the loom with the cross resting on the breast beam and the loops which were around peg A hanging down on the far side of it. See, however, portee cross, page 63.

2. Insert two very smooth sticks called *lease sticks,* provided with the loom, through the cross exactly where pegs B and C were. You can find the place easily because of the ties which you made at a, b, c, and d, of warping frame or reel. Tie the ends of these sticks together *securely* through the holes there for this purpose, keeping the sticks about two-finger-widths apart. Check to make sure that the lease sticks are exactly where they should be, then remove the four original ties of the cross.

3. Quite often the distance from the cross to the end of the loops hanging down is too short. If it is less than about 12 inches, the loops will pull out of the reed while you are working so the cross will have to be moved down the warp. The easiest way to do this is to have someone hold the warp chain taut at the brake tie while you take those warp ends which are coming over the lease stick next to the end of the warp in one hand and the others in the other hand. Pull your hands apart and as you do so the cross will peel back as far as needed, taking the lease sticks with it. Do not, under any circumstances, untie or remove the lease sticks. The necessity for moving the cross can be eliminated if you make your own warping equipment and see that the distance between peg A and where the cross is made is about twelve or fifteen inches.

4. Tie or clamp the lease sticks to the top of the breast beam in such a manner that the warp ends can still be moved along them.

5. Where the brake tie comes (this should be at or near the floor) tie a heavy cord around the warp chain and then tie the chain to the heel bar of the loom, or if you have a table loom, tie a weight to the warp chain. This puts a tension on the warp to facilitate the spreading through the reed.

6. Remove the reed of your loom from the beater and lay it flat upon two narrow boards which you have placed, one to each side, from slabstock to breast beam of your loom. To do this you will need to push the heddles aside. If this warp were a very wide one, the harnesses themselves would have to be removed from the loom and laid aside temporarily.

7. Locate the center of the reed, and tie on a short bit of string to mark the spot permanently or daub on some colored nail polish.

8. Measure off to the right of this mark seven and one-half inches which is the point where the spreading will begin in order to center the 15-inch width in the reed. If you are left-handed, it will probably be better for you to start the spreading at the

same distance to the left of center. The reed to be used for this warp is a 15-dent reed. Most reeds are marked at one end or the other with the dentage.

9. Select *at the cross where two by two the warp ends go over and under the lease sticks,* the first eight warp ends on the right (or left, if you are left-handed). Put these eight warp ends (two complete loops) through that dent of the reed which is 7½ inches to the right (or left) of the center, using the *draw-in hook* provided with your loom. (See Illustration 12.) Bring the

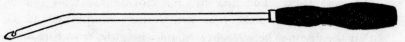

Illustration 12.   A draw-in hook.

hook up from underneath the reed through this dent. Loop the ends around this hook and pull them back to the underside. There is an S-shaped plastic reed hook which I prefer to use for this purpose, because the handle of the draw-in hook makes it awkward to use. This S-shaped hook can easily be made at home though any weaving supply house has them. (See Illustration 13.) A silver knife will also work well by laying the warp ends

Illustration 13.   A reed hook (actual size).

across the dent to be filled and pushing them down through the reed with its blade.

Perhaps the two extra warp ends which were tied originally around peg A are at the side of the warp where you have begun. If so, add them to the eight already in the dent.

10. Continue to spread the warp in the reed by skipping the next

three dents towards the center of the reed. In the fourth dent place eight more warp ends (two complete loops). *Always select the warp ends at the cross so that you are certain to take them in their strict order. Pay no attention to the way the warp ends may be twisted beyond the lease sticks, it is the cross which is keeping them in their correct order.* Skip three more dents, put eight warp ends in the next; skip three, eight in the next, etc., all the way across the width of the warp.

You will find it easier to select the correct warp ends at the lease sticks if you pull on the loops of the warp with one hand while doing so, and also if you spread out the warp ends along the sticks.

Perhaps there is a mistake in the cross which you have just discovered, so that at one place four warp ends are lying side by side instead of two. Put all four of them in one dent together with four others, to make up the eight. Later on when you are threading your warp ends in the heddles, you will learn what to do with these four ends.

When you have completed the spreading of the warp ends as above, there will be 30 warp ends in each inch of the reed though, of course, they are bunched. If you find that you have made a few mistakes in counting out the dents in this spreading, it is of no importance. It is important, however, that you select the warp ends at the lease sticks in their correct order.

The sole object of spreading the warp in this way by placing several warp ends in one dent and then skipping dents is to get the warp spread out to a fifteen-inch width as quickly as possible. It would be a waste of time to put two warp ends through each dent at this stage in the procedure because this spreading is only a temporary one and the warp will be removed from the reed as soon as it is wound on the warp beam. In addition, to put two warp ends through each dent would necessitate cutting the loops.

Naturally, you will not always wish to use a 15-dent reed. Suppose you are using a warp planned to have 12 warp ends per inch. You might use a 12-dent reed. To spread this warp you could put four warp ends through a dent (one loop); skip three dents. Put four warp ends through the next dent and skip three dents, etc., all the way across. Fifteen- and twelve-dent reeds are the ones most commonly used by weavers, but you can, of course, use whatever size you have available for this spreading. If you cannot make the arithmetic "come out right," it is better to spread the warp a little wider in the reed than needed rather than narrower.

As for myself, I use for the spreading of all warps—no matter how many ends per inch—a reed bought especially for the purpose which has only four dents in each inch. (An exception will be noted in the discussion of a warp wound with the use of a paddle.) I poke loops (I never cut them) through the dents and skip a dent whenever I think it is necessary, just so that the warp is spread out to approximately the width I need, and preferably an inch or two wider.

In place of a reed, you may also use what is called a *raddle*. A raddle resembles a wide rake, the teeth of which are vertical pegs or finishing nails. The distance between the pegs is usually one-half inch. Some raddles are made to fit into the grooves of the beater, and after the spreading is done, the top of the beater comes down over the pegs and prevents the warp ends from pulling out. Others have a top which is hinged at one side so that it can be lowered over the pegs. This type must be fastened in some way to the loom uprights as shown in Illustration 14. Raddles can be purchased, but they are not hard for a do-it-yourself person to make. In the description which follows, the word *reed* could also mean *raddle*.

11. All the loops hanging from the underside of the reed must now be placed on a smooth stick . . . a yard stick does well for this. In placing the looped warp ends on this stick, it is very important to make sure that they are not twisted. *In other words, those warp ends which are going over the lease stick next to the reed must be on top of this smooth stick*. Take care, also, to tie on to this stick any incomplete loops there may be at either side of the warp. Now fasten this stick in some way temporarily so that it cannot fall out of the loops.

12. Go to the rear of the loom and unwind the apron from the warp
beam and bring it up over the slabstock of the loom. Aprons,
both those on the warp and the cloth beam, are provided with
apron sticks that are either threaded through the deeply notched
hems of the aprons or attached to them by means of tapes or

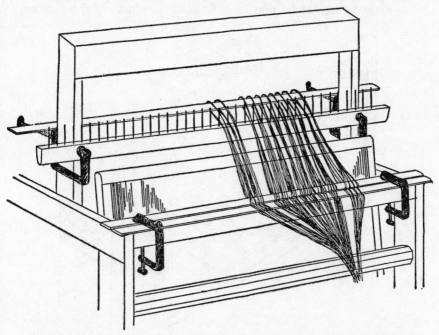

Illustration 14. Spreading the warp. A raddle is being used with pegs one-
half inch apart. In order to show the warp ends clearly, the pegs were not drawn
as long as they actually are.

cords. See Illustrations 15 and 16. If the beams of your loom do
not have aprons, you can staple three long doubled cords to
them, putting one at each side and one in the middle of each
beam and these will take their place. The ends of the cords
are looped around the apron sticks as shown in Illustration 17.
Aprons should be several inches wider than the weaving
capacity of your loom, and long enough to reach up over the
beams and halfway (at least) to the harnesses.

13. Now that the spreading in the reed has been done, it is a good thing to take the trouble to recount your warp ends while they are bunched just in case you have miscounted in winding them. Unless the variance is very great, it can be taken care of later when the pattern is being threaded. If you have omitted so many warp ends that the finished product will be much

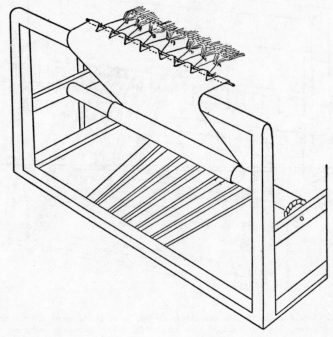

Illustration 15. An apron stick is put through the deeply notched hem of the apron.

narrower than you had planned on, stop here and wind extra ones in the same way that you wound the original ones. Make the cross, tie it as before and chain off the warp. Slip this additional warp on to your lease sticks, one end of which will have to be untied to admit them. Retie the lease sticks. Spread these new ends through the reed, and you are ready to go on.

The warp will not be exactly centered in the reed, but perhaps you can push the reed along the groove if there is room. At any rate, this cannot be helped now.

On the other hand, if you have wound too many warp ends, you can eliminate them, if you wish, simply by pulling them out of the reed.

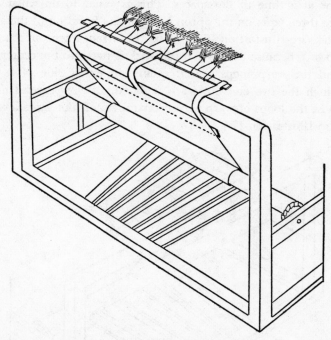

Illustration 16. Another method of attaching apron stick to hem of apron.

14. Put the reed back in the beater. The raddle stays in place, its pegs either covered by the top of the beater or its own hinged top.
15. Untie the warp from the heel bar, remove the brake tie and unclamp the lease sticks from the breast beam.
16. Draw the stick holding the loops of warp towards the rear of the loom. An assistant can be of great help here, for the warp

should be held taut in front. You will probably need to push the lease sticks away from the reed along the warp to make the loops long enough to reach the rear.

17. Transfer the loops on the yardstick to the apron stick of the warp beam. The apron stick will, of course, have to be taken out of the lacing or hem of the apron and the loops placed a few at a time in the spaces. This is easier to do when there are three tapes on the apron hem for the insertion of the apron stick (see Illustration 16, showing this arrangement on the front apron), because then the apron stick is put into the center tape and the warp loops spaced evenly on either side of it after which the two end tapes are replaced. Be very careful not to twist the loops of warp as you take them off the yardstick. (See also Illustration 17.)

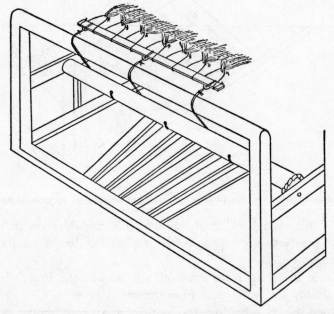

Illustration 17. Doubled cords from the cloth (or the warp) beam can be used to take the place of an apron. These doubled cords must all be the same length so that the apron stick is parallel to the breast beam.

18. With the warp held taut in front, trace the loops from the reed back to the apron stick with your fingers separating them on the apron stick to see that they are not unduly piled up one on the other and that they come in a straight line from the dents. The width of the warp on the apron stick should be made the same as it is in the reed, or a few inches wider. You now have the warp spaced on the apron stick of the warp beam; the warp is being held taut in front and the lease sticks are in front of the reed. The following steps show how to transfer the lease sticks and the cross from the front of the reed to the rear without losing the cross.

19. Move the lease sticks up close to the reed. Turn the one which is nearer the reed on edge, flat against the partitions. Look behind the reed and you will see a little tunnel formed there in the warp. With the warp held taut, thrust through this narrow opening another smooth stick, a lease stick is best if you have one, taking care that it does not catch up any of the warp ends which are on either the top or the bottom of the tunnel. Draw this stick to the rear of the loom and tie it at each side to the slabstock so it cannot fall out. You will quickly see that this stick is separating the upper and lower layer of the warp exactly the same as the apron stick is, and it is, therefore, a check on your work.

20. Untie the ends of the two lease sticks in front of the reed and remove the one that you just turned on edge . . . *the one near the reed.*

21. Push the remaining front lease stick up to the reed so that it is on edge with its flat side against the reed. Hold it there securely while your assistant shakes the warp gently. It may even be necessary to give the warp a few quick spanks with the flat side of another smooth stick both in front and behind the reed, but be careful lest the lease stick at the reed fall out. Keep the warp taut, and the warp ends behind the reed will again separate into a little tunnel. Into this carefully insert a lease stick, *making certain that those warp ends which are on top of*

the lease stick at the front of the reed are also on top of this stick which you are inserting. In other words, the new lease stick must go through the tunnel without picking up any of the warp ends from the bottom of the tunnel.

22. Push this new lease stick back to the other one tied at the rear and tie the two together through holes in the ends of them just as the original lease sticks were tied. Remove the remaining front lease stick from the warp. The cross is now at the rear of the loom in perfect order just as before.

    While it is true that some weavers do not transfer the cross until later on when the warp has been wound on the warp beam, it has been my experience that students are likely to forget about it with disastrous results. So better do it now!

The warp is now ready to be beamed or wound on the warp beam.

BEAMING THE WARP

This method of beaming a warp requires the assistance of at least one other person, and in my classes we are in the habit of calling this person "Horsey." Horsey must hold the warp so that it is taut and must pay special attention to the selvages (outer warp ends) to see that they are not slack. Here is the procedure:

1. While Horsey holds the chain of warp, it is untied and un-chained for the entire length of the room—the more the better in the case of a cotton warp. Some fibers, especially linen, need to be put on the beam more gradually, however. The warp is then kept taut, shaken out well and, if there are still in-equalities, it is spanked *hard* with a smooth flat stick using the flat side to strike the warp. Yes, the warp is actually spanked across the width of it! You will be surprised how this makes a warp behave. Let the reed or raddle in the beater lean against the breast beam. If the raddle is of the type that must be tied to the loom uprights, then, of course, it remains there with its hinged top securely in place.

2. Start cranking the warp beam. Most looms require that you wind towards the rear or clockwise, but check carefully the instructions sent with yours. If you have nothing to guide you, wind on a few inches and put the catch on the ratchet of the warp beam. Then pull on the warp from the front of the loom and if it is wound correctly the catch will prevent the warp from unwinding.

3. Watch those lease sticks! They must not disappear down over the slabstock and get wound in the warp. Keep pushing them back towards the harnesses every once in a while.

4. Horsey must hold the warp half in one hand, half in the other, and hold it so that the tension feels even all across the width. Horsey also stands directly in line with the center of the reed or raddle.

5. As soon as the apron stick begins to wind on the warp beam, place over it a sheet of paper upon which the warp can wind. Do not use newspaper as it is not tough enough but the large garment bags from the dry cleaner's are excellent for the purpose. They must be cut several inches wider than the warp, for you must always have a good margin of paper extending beyond the edge of the warp. It is better to use short lengths of paper as longer pieces tend to wind on spirally, becoming wider at one side of the beam and too narrow at the other. With a cotton warp it is safe to make one or two revolutions of the beam with no paper between. Insert another sheet of paper, keeping it smooth and unwrinkled. Some weavers use old blueprints for this purpose and flat, smooth sticks like yardsticks are also satisfactory being inserted at the rate of about four sticks to a revolution.

Separating the layers of warp in this manner is necessary because otherwise the warp ends will sink into the previous layer, making ridges as the warp is wound. Each ridge changes the circumference of the beam, making differences in the tension of the various warp ends.

6. As the warp is beamed, Horsey exerts a pull on it and gradually

is more or less pulled toward the reed. The warp ends must not slip through Horsey's fingers but be held firmly. Considerable tension is thus put on a cotton warp though a wool warp would be put on much more lightly.

7. When Horsey arrives near the reed, he or she lets go of the warp, unchains more of it and shakes it out. Then the warp is spanked again and the winding continues. All during the beaming Horsey keeps an eye on the beater, for if it starts to move backward, the beaming must stop immediately until the tangles there are straightened out. Sometimes in spite of all precautions, bad tangles do occur in front of the reed or raddle. Have near at hand, therefore, a fairly stiff scrubbing brush and if the tangles will not spank out, brush them towards Horsey who then grasps the loose ends and draws them back. When the warp is smooth for as long a distance as possible, wind on a little more, then brush again. Brushing is not recommended except when there are many tangles and should never be done in the case of a wool warp. Usually these tangles result from not keeping the tension uniform during the preparation of the warp on the frame or reel, and it requires patience to beam such a warp, but it can be done.

8. If a warp end should break during the beaming, tie the ends of it together again, inserting a short piece of the warp yarn, if necessary, to make it long enough. Later on in the weaving, all knots in the warp must be eliminated by treating them as if they were broken warp ends. (Page 93.)

9. Beam on the warp until the looped ends in Horsey's hands reach the reed. Now tie the lease sticks to the slabstock so that they cannot fall down.

10. Take a few of the loops in front of the reed and cut them. Pull them out of the reed and tie them together in a slip knot near the lease sticks. (See Illustration 18, slip knot.) Continue to cut and tie in groups until all have been removed from the reed.

11. The reed or the raddle can now be removed from the loom and

laid aside, for you are ready to thread your pattern. See Chapter 6.

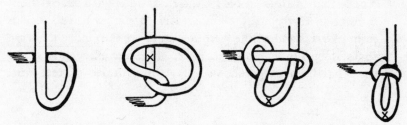

Illustration 18. Slip knot. After the loop is made as shown on the left, the fingers reach down into this loop, take hold at x and pull it through.

BEAMING WITHOUT AN ASSISTANT

Happy is the weaver who has an assistant, not all of us are so lucky! Do not be dismayed, however, for beaming can be done alone.

That part of the process which particularly requires the aid of another person, not necessarily a weaver, is the holding of the warp at a tension while it is being cranked on the plain beam. It takes a little "know-how" to beam a warp alone, but the following method has proved satisfactory time and time again for me:

1. Take a heavy cardboard carton and near the bottom of one side punch a hole large enough to slip the end of the chain of warp through. In this carton place a weight. The floors of my classroom are made of a slippery composition material, and the looms are heavy ones so I need two old varnish cans filled with sand, each one weighing sixteen pounds. The weight needed, of course, varies with the nature of the floor or its covering, the warp fiber, and the loom.

2. Spread the warp through the reed or raddle as outlined on the previous pages, and have it all ready for beaming.

3. Take the chain of warp coming from the front of the reed or raddle and insert the whole thing through the hole in the side of the box. Unravel as much of the chain as you wish and

inside the box place a shuttle or smooth stick through the last loop of the chain to prevent it from unravelling any farther.

4. Notice that in Illustration 19, the lease sticks have not yet been transferred to the rear. Many weavers prefer to leave them in front like this and, as the warp is wound on, they move the lease sticks along the length of the warp. It works excellently if the warp has been prepared on the warping frame or reel with

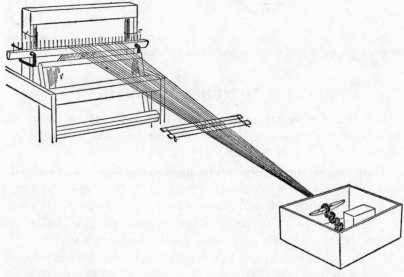

Illustration 19. Apparatus used for beaming a plain beam without an assistant. The lease sticks have not yet been transferred to the rear, and the top for the raddle is not shown.

care to keep the tension even. But I am always afraid that I will forget to transfer the cross before I cut the loops when the beaming is completed, so I make a practice of transferring the cross as described. Of course, if a raddle is used instead of a reed for the spreading, all you have to do, after the beaming is finished, is to lift off the top of the raddle and remove it. The lease sticks, holding the cross, can then be pushed to the rear of the loom. This is the big advantage of using a raddle.

5. Place the box on the floor far enough from the loom so that the warp is stretched out taut and untwisted. Feel the warp and

then move the box from one side to the other until both the selvages and the middle of the warp have the same tension.

6. Wind on the warp as usual, dragging the box, weight, and all across the floor. Unwind some more of the warp chain and continue, always checking the tension from time to time. While this does require considerable going backwards and forwards from back to front of the loom many times, a warp winds on surprisingly easily this way. The last yard or so is the hardest. To help with this part, you can remove the breast beam from the loom, and when the box works up close to the loom, it is sometimes a good idea to put it on a chair, and pull box, chair and all, in order to finish the job.

Wide warps are prepared in two halves and chained off separately. (See page 30.) In this case, one chain is placed in one box and the other in another box. A pair of lease sticks is used with each chain. See that you have the same weight in each box and that the tension of each is uniform.

That's all there is to it!

BEAMING A WARP PREPARED WITH THE USE OF A PADDLE

A warp which has both a porrey cross and a portee cross (see Chapter 3) presents certain deviations in the procedure of beaming which are included in the following directions:

1. Place a pair of lease sticks through the second or portee cross at the places previously occupied by pegs I and J of the warping board or the corresponding pegs of a reel. Tie the lease sticks as usual and remove the ties made at the cross.

2. Put the raddle in place. It may fit into the groove of the beater or be fastened to the loom uprights, whichever is suitable. Fold over the top of the raddle's rakelike projections a piece of heavy paper.

3. Bring the lease sticks to the rear of the loom over the top of the raddle, having first pushed the heddles out of the way.

4. Take the apron stick and thread it alternately through the first tab of the apron hem on the warp beam then through a group

of the loops at the end of the warp, then through another tab of the apron and through more loops of warp until the warp ends are all evenly distributed on the apron. This is the same procedure as described in (17) on page 56.

5. Tie the warp chain at the heel bar on the floor level in front of the loom so that the unchained part of the warp is at a tension.

6. Remove the paper from the raddle and push the lease sticks up about halfway towards it from the slabstock.

7. Place the groups of warp ends coming by sixes (or whatever the number of warp ends you used with the paddle) into the spaces of the raddle. Be sure you do not cross them as they come from the lease sticks to the raddle. See that the warp is centered in the raddle and that it is spread out to the width desired or, better still, to an inch or two wider. You may need to place two groups of six in some spaces or to skip spaces in order to do this spreading.

8. Place the top on the raddle.

9. Check to see that the warp ends on the apron stick are spaced out to the same width as they are in the raddle.

10. Unfasten the warp chain from the heel bar and also any other ties made in the warp at the time it was prepared.

11. Wind the warp on the warp beam with paper or thin slats between the layers as is your custom. Some weavers allow the lease sticks to be wound on with the warp, others push them ahead.

12. When the first or porrey cross comes up to the raddle in front, the lease sticks behind the raddle are removed if they have not been allowed to go on the warp beam.

13. Insert lease sticks in the porrey cross just as usual.

14. Remove the raddle from the loom. Push the lease sticks back to the slabstock and tie them there.

15. Cut the loops of warp and tie them into small groups using a slip knot. This completes the beaming, and the loom is ready for threading.

Chapter 6

THREADING THE PATTERN, SLEYING THE REED, AND LACING ON THE WARP TO THE CLOTH BEAM

While I feel sure that anyone who has a loom and has woven on it will know how to thread a pattern, the new weaver will need this information. In the first place, a weaving pattern is known as a *draft,* and, for some reason unknown to me, drafts are read from right to left. Here is what a draft looks like. It is for a small pattern called *Rose Path* which is suitable both for borders and for all-over pattern weaving.

ROSE PATH

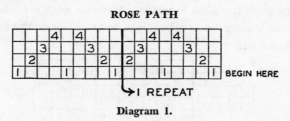

Diagram 1.

As a weaver sits in front of the loom, the harness before him or her is called the first harness, and they are numbered in order from front to back. Some looms, as has already been said, have more than four harnesses while some have only two.

In a weaving draft the numbers between the lines (though sometimes x's or oblique lines are used instead of figures) refer to harness numbers and indicate that a warp end is to be threaded through a heddle on that harness. Frequently squared paper is used for draft writing.

However, before you can actually start to thread your warp in the Rose Path draft, there is some paper work which you must do in order to fit the draft into the number of warp ends you have wound.

Rose Path is a very small draft with but eight warp ends in each repeat of the design (Diagram 1). Inasmuch as the warp you have prepared has 458 warp ends in it, 8 of which were reserved for the selvages (page 20), you have available 450 warp ends for the draft itself.

Divide the number of warp ends required for one repeat of the draft (8) into this number and you will find that there can be 56 repeats of the draft in the total of 450 warp ends plus two warp ends left over. Do not ignore these two warp ends for, to make your calculations come out even, one of them will be used at the beginning of each selvage. Selvages are generally threaded 1, 2, 3 and 4 for the right hand selvage and reversed, 4, 3, 2, 1 for the left. For a selvage which is not written in this manner, you might like to turn to page 133 to see the draft given there. It is a special instance, however, and not applicable here.

Now the draft for Rose Path looks like this with the selvages and the two extra warp ends taken into account: Remember to read from right to left.

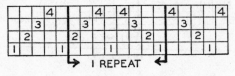

I REPEAT

Diagram 2.

Let us thread this draft together. Some weavers prefer to sit at the rear of the loom to thread, others in front. When two people work together, the one in back hands the warp ends to the one in front of the loom who then threads them. It is easier for the one in front if the breast beam is removed.

To facilitate the threading, you will find it well to write down the figures in the draft in lines so that you can read them in the customary manner from left to right like this:

Line A. 4.1.2.3.4. (1 extra warp end plus selvage)   5 warp ends used
Line B. 1.2.3.4.1.4.3.2. (Repeat 56 times; 8 × 56)   448 "   "   "
Line C. 1 (This is the end of the last pattern repeat
    which makes it balance with the first repeat
    which begins on harness 1. It also uses up your
    other extra warp end.)   1   "   "   "
Line D. 4.3.2.1. (Selvage)   4   "   "   "
                            Total   458   "   "   "

If you found when a recount was made on page 54 that you have a few more than 458 warp ends, the selvages can be further increased. Suppose you have two extra warp ends or 460 in all. Line A would then read 3.4.1.2.3.4 and line D would read 4.3.2.1.4. It is not correct drafting (except as noted in Part 2) to have figure 1 follow figure 3 or figure 2 follow figure 4 or to have two identical figures one after the other, such as two 1's and this is the reason why the enlarged selvage in line A begins as it does. The explanation of why this has to be done is given in Chapter 8 for such threadings form what is there described as a *flat*.

Place the above data somewhere on your loom—one copy at the rear and one in front if two people are working together so that they can check on each other. There are three procedures to follow now depending upon the type of warp beam you are using:

THREADING THE PLAIN BEAM

1. Take the first two warp ends of the cross *at the lease sticks* (left-hand side of the loom as you sit at the rear). Separate the two cut ends but do not remove them from the lease sticks.

Put one of them (either one) through the first heddle of harness
number 4 which, you will remember, is the harness at the rear
of the loom. Put the other one through the first heddle of
harness number 1 (see line A). (If your warp was prepared with
a paddle, you will find that the warp ends are separated one
by one instead of two by two at the lease sticks.) If you are
working by yourself, simply use your fingers and thread the
warp end through the eye of the designated heddle. When you
have an assistant at the front of the loom, hold the heddle while
your helper puts the long-handled draw-in hook through the
eye of it. Loop the warp end over the hook after which it is
drawn through to the front of the loom. The warp ends should
be long enough so that they will not be pulled out again acci-
dentally and some of the warp's length may have to be un-
wound from the warp beam to accomplish this. As each heddle
is threaded, it is pushed over to your left.

2. Select the next two warp ends at the cross as before, separate
   them and put one through the eye of the first heddle of harness
   number 2 and the other through the first heddle of harness
   number 3.

3. Select two more warp ends, making sure that they are the next
   two of the cross. Take one of these and put it through the
   eye of the second heddle of harness 4. When you sit at the rear
   of the loom you are thus threading the heddles from left to
   right one after the other using the harnesses called for in the
   draft. The threading of these first five warp ends completes
   Line A, page 67. Tie these five warp ends in a slip knot in front
   of harness 1.

4. Put warp end number 6 through the eye of the second heddle of
   harness 1 and continue to thread line B, always selecting the
   warp ends where they cross over and under the lease sticks.
   All drafts are threaded in this same manner.

5. When you have threaded four repeats of the draft, tie all these
   warp ends into one slip knot in front of harness 1. Now check
   your threading. In these four repeats there should be eight

heddles threaded on each of the four harnesses (not counting the five ends of the selvage, line A). Make any corrections necessary before continuing with the threading. It does not matter if you have left a heddle empty by mistake just as long as the required 32 heddles are correctly threaded. Check also to make sure that you have not omitted any warp ends at the cross and, of course, ascertain that they have been chosen in their correct order.

6. Now count off the next eight heddles on each of the four harnesses and tie off all the others. This will be a check on your threading of the next four repeats. The warp ends already threaded are tied with a slip knot. You must not make a single mistake in the threading or it will have to be redone, so constant checking is essential.

7. When you have threaded the 56 repeats of line B, follow the directions of line C by threading the next warp end to a heddle on harness 1 which balances the first repeat of the Rose Path draft.

8. Finally, thread line D, the other selvage, and if you have threaded and counted correctly, this will use up all your warp ends.

9. If you have made an error anywhere in the forming of the cross when the warp was being prepared there will be at that place four warp ends lying side by side at the lease sticks instead of the usual two. The only thing to do is to select them in the order which you think is correct. This may mean that these four warp ends will become twisted around one another for the entire length of the warp so that they may have to be untwisted by hand as the warp is moved forward when weaving. This is the reason why only two warp ends were used at a time in the preparation of the warp in Chapter 3.

THREADING THE SECTIONAL BEAM

When a warp has been beamed sectionally, the method of threading is essentially the same except for the fact that there are no lease sticks and no cross made. A sectional beam is threaded as follows:

1. Unpin the tapes from all the sections and reverse the warp beam until the warp strands are long enough so that when they come up and *over* the slabstock to be threaded through the heddles they will hang down in front about 8 inches. Then by means of masking tape fasten each section of the warp to the upper part of the loom in the rear, i.e., rear of roller *V* in the frontispiece, making very sure that none of them is twisted from the section. The pencilled "X" marks which you made on the tape on which the warp ends are stuck will help guide you.

2. Begin to thread the first section at the left of the rear of the loom by pulling off the first warp end on the left of the tape and threading it exactly as was described for the plain beam loom. Follow with the second, third, and fourth warp ends, etc., selecting them *in the exact order* in which they were gummed in place. Take care not to twist the ribbon of warp as it comes from the section at any time during the threading. When the first section is threaded, continue with the next until all are threaded.

3. If you should make a mistake in the threading making it necessary to pull warp ends out of the heddles, remember you have no cross so be sure to stick them on to a piece of masking tape for re-threading.

4. From here on everything is the same for either type of beam.

THREADING THE READY-SPOOLED WARP BEAM

Many of the table looms are equipped with a warp beam which is a hexagonal steel rod upon which spools of warp purchased already wound are slipped. Some floor looms have these beams as extra equipment.

On the face of it, it would look as if this type of beam would be a very great advantage to have and, as far as being a labor and time-saver, it is. These beams are therefore commonly used in schools and for Occupational Therapy. However, the yarns which may be purchased on ready-warped spools are limited to a very few:

carpet warp, 20/2 cotton, and 40/2 linen and they entail quite an outlay of money.

If your loom has this sort of beam, place each spool on it un-opened with the arrow pointing toward the front of the loom and with all the arrows lined up. Break the seals on the spools and bring the warp up over the slabstock, unwinding enough from the spools to reach through to the front of the loom. Then fasten each ribbon of warp to the rear of the loom at the top. Each spool represents a two-inch width of warp in a 15-dent reed. The thread-ing is similar to that of a sectionally wound warp, for you begin at the left spool on the beam at the rear of the loom and thread each warp end of each spool one after the other as you take them off the gummed tape. The amount wound off from each spool must be exactly the same.

When you buy warp wound on these spools, there are sixty warp ends on each spool of the 20/2 cotton and the 40/2 linen warp and thirty ends per spool of the carpet warp. Spools may be purchased in either the ten or the twenty yard length. The smallest looms using this type of warp are the 8-inch "Structo" looms which hold four spools of warp. Because many people have these small looms, it would be wise to figure out a warp plan just this wide for the Rose Path draft, using the 20/2 cotton.

Four spools each with sixty warp ends means a total of 240 warp ends. The Rose Path draft, having 8 warp ends in each repeat of it, will fit into this total number 29 times with exactly 8 warp ends left for selvages. Thread the first selvage 1.2.3.4 just as was done before on page 66 and write it all down in lines like this:

Line A. 1.2.3.4…selvage	4 warp ends used	
Line B. 1.2.3.4.1.4.3.2…repeat 29 times (29 × 8)	232 " " "	
Line C. 1…to balance the draft	1 " " "	
Line D. 4.3.2…other selvage	3 " " "	
Total	240 " " "	

The second selvage is reduced by one warp end, but this is im-material.

Many table looms hold ten spools though the loom does not have to be warped to its full capacity. If you wish to use on such a loom the 458 warp ends as planned originally in Chapter 2, put eight spools of warp on the hexagonal beam and follow the threading given on page 67. Part of the last spool will not be used. These unthreaded warp ends must be cut off from time to time as weaving progresses for they get in the way.

SLEYING THE REED

After the threading by any method is completed, the warp ends are again put through the reed, this time to stay. This process is called *sleying*. Place your 15-dent reed upon two narrow boards placed from front to rear of the loom so that the reed is flat and parallel to the breast beam as it was during the spreading. This is the way to sley a warp through the reed:

1. Take the first two warp ends that you threaded and put them through that dent of the reed which is $7\frac{1}{2}$ inches from its center. Start at this distance because the warp must be centered in the reed and it was planned to be 15 inches wide. If you are left-handed, perhaps it would be easier if you started at the other side of the warp.

2. Take the next two warp ends and put them through the next dent towards the center of the reed. *Do not skip dents.* The draw-in or reed hook, the S-shaped hook or the blade of a table knife can be used when sleying a reed in the same manner as described in Chapter 5.

3. Continue to select the warp ends by twos, placing two in each dent of the reed. Make sure that the warp ends are not crossed or twisted as they exit from the heddle eyes.

4. Every inch or so pull on the warp ends hanging down under the reed and inspect your work closely, making certain that there are no skipped dents and that each dent has two, and only two, warp ends in it. It will certainly save you a great deal of time to be careful now to get the sleying correct.

5. Tie the ends underneath the reed about every two inches in slip knots so they cannot pull out.

6. When the warp is sleyed all across, replace the reed in the beater with all the slip-knotted ends hanging down in front of it. Fasten the top of the beater over the reed. There are now in the reed thirty ends of warp per inch.

LACING ON THE WARP

The next step is to fasten the warp ends coming from the reed to the apron stick as follows:

1. Take the first bunch of warp ends and untie them. Gently stroke the warp ends towards you to pull out inequalities in the

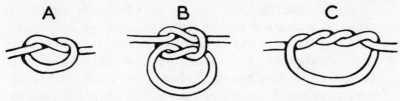

Illustration 20. A. Overhand knot. B. Square knot. C. Beginning of the surgeon's knot.

tension. Look to see that they are all smooth where they come through the lease sticks behind the harnesses, or from the sections of a sectional beam (making sure none is caught around a peg), or from the ready-warped spools. If the latter, it is wise to use a brush to smooth out the warp at the spools where it may have piled up during the threading. Then retie the bunch of warp ends with a hard knot close to the cut ends, and do likewise with the next bunch and so on. These bunches do not necessarily need to have the same number of warp ends in them. In fact, it is well to have about one-half an inch (as measured in the reed) at the beginning and ending of the sleying to assure good tension for the outside edges while the other bunches can measure about an inch and a half in the reed. Try not to split the ends which are together in a dent by tying them in different bunches. These knots do not need to be in perfect alignment, either, for the next step will take care of that. (The bunches of warp ends are also called *bouts*.)

2. Take a piece of strong cord about three times as long as the width of the warp and begin to lace the bunches of warp on to the apron stick of the cloth beam by tying it first to the right hand side of the stick near where the first bunch of the warp ends will be as it comes straight from the reed. The apron stick should be about three or four inches from the breast beam.

3. Bring this cord from above down through the center of the first bunch of warp ends at the right side of the warp. Then bring the end of the cord under the apron stick and up over it and then down into the middle of the next bunch of warp ends, pulling the cord and holding it so that these two bunches are held taut. There should be about two inches left between the apron stick and the knot of each bunch to allow for later adjustment. The three figures which show the methods of attaching an apron stick to the apron (see Illustrations 15, 16, and 17) also show the lacing on of the warp. These sketches are idealized, for we do not often get the knots at the end of a warp in quite such an even row.

4. When all bunches have been laced on, adjust the tension across the entire warp by pulling on the cord between the bunches until your sense of touch tells you that the tension is the same. This is most important, and care should be taken that no part of the warp feels tighter or slacker than the rest, after which the lacing cord is tied at the left-hand side of the apron stick.

5. The lease sticks which are still in place behind the harnesses can be left there, tied loosely to the slabstock, or they may be removed entirely. However, if you intend to change the threading of this warp before it is all used up, then the lease sticks which are holding the warp ends in order would better be left in place. There is no cross in a warp wound sectionally or

on ready-warped spools, therefore, no lease sticks. To learn how to insert them, should you ever desire to re-thread your warp, continue to read on and then follow the instructions which are given on page 90.

Chapter 7

TYING UP THE TREADLES

Before any weaving can be done on a floor loom, the treadles must be tied up in order to operate the harnesses. Most floor looms have six treadles. Above these are four levers which are called *lamms,* and above the lamms are the four harnesses. (See Chapter 1.)

Each harness is fastened to the center of the lamm beneath it with cord, using a snitch knot (see Illustration 21), or with hooks.

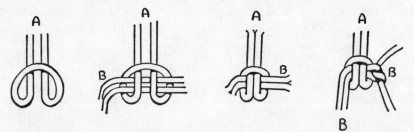

Illustration 21. The snitch knot. A. Ends from lamm; B. Ends from treadle.

When the lamms have been tied or fastened to the harnesses, they should be in a horizontal position with respect to the floor and the harnesses, themselves, together with the lower and top rollers (U and V) must be level. Next the lamms, in turn, are tied to the treadles so that by stepping on the treadles the harnesses are put into motion. The tie-up, therefore, is from treadle to lamm to harness.

The system used to tie up the treadles varies with the weave, but for a simple draft such as Rose Path and indeed for many, many others, including the old coverlet patterns and all the overshots, there are two main systems in use today. The first of these (Diagram 3) is the one preferred by Mrs. Mary M. Atwater, whose text *The Shuttle-Craft Book of American Hand-Weaving* has been a standard for many years.

NOTE: Part Two of this book explains the above references to *weaves* and *overshots*.

THE ATWATER TIE-UP

Explanation of Diagram 3

Begin at the first treadle on the left (as you face the front of the loom) which in this instance is called treadle number 1. Through a screw eye on this treadle (the first screw eye towards the front) run the loop of a doubled length of cord. Draw its ends through its own loop, thus securing the cord in the screw eye. Tie another length of cord into a loop long enough to

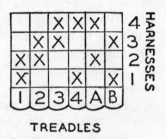

TREADLES (FRONT OF LOOM)

Diagram 3.

come halfway down from the first lamm to the floor. You will soon find out whether this cord is the right length once the knot to be described is tied. Fasten this doubled cord into the screw eye on this first lamm—the screw eye which is directly above the treadle. Bend the loop back upon the two strands of this cord coming from the lamm, then take the two ends coming from the treadle, and insert them into this loop. (See Illustration 21.) When these two ends have been tied together in a simple overhand knot, you have completed what is known as the *snitch* or *loom knot*. This knot seems to be unique to the weaver's craft. It does not jam under tension and can easily be adjusted up or down by untying and adjusting the overhand knot. When you were hanging the harnesses and followed the directions given in Chapter 1, you also used this snitch knot.

The angle at which the treadles are tied up from the floor should be such that, when operated with the feet, the treadles sink a distance equal to half the length of one of your heddles. The snitch knot, being easily adjusted, allows you to tie the treadles temporarily now and to change the angle later if necessary. Remember that while the treadles are being tied up, the lamms, the harnesses, and rollers above them must be kept level and horizontal.

To continue with the explanation of Mrs. Atwater's tie-up: Put another doubled cord through the next screw eye of treadle number 1 and tie it also by means of the snitch knot to the second lamm using that screw eye or hook on this lamm which is directly in line with the one on the first lamm. Treadle number 1 (first on the left) has now been tied to lamms 1 and 2, which means that it is also indirectly tied to harnesses 1 and 2. This is what is indicated by the two x's on treadle 1 of Diagram 3.

Treadle number 2, as shown by the x's, is tied to lamms 2 and 3; treadle number 3 to lamms 3 and 4 and so on, twelve knots being needed in all. In this tie-up, treadles A and B are the ones that are used to weave without pattern in what is known as *plain weave* or *tabby*. Treadles 1, 2 and 3 are operated one at a time with the left foot and the others with the right.

MR. WORST'S TIE-UP OR, AS IT IS MOST OFTEN REFERRED TO, THE WORST TIE-UP

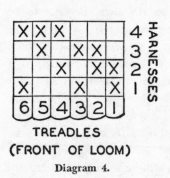

TREADLES
(FRONT OF LOOM)

Diagram 4.

Explanation of Diagram 4

Diagram 4 shows the tie-up given by Edward F. Worst in his book entitled *Foot-Power Loom Weaving*. The same knot is used, but the treadles are numbered from right to left and the tabby treadles are in the middle (numbers 3 and 4).

One system is as good as the other.

My classes use the Worst tie-up because it seems easier to alternate the feet when weaving tabby. In Mr. Worst's tie-up treadles 1, 2, and 3 are operated one at a time with the right foot and the others with the left. (See Illustration 22.)

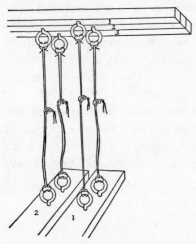

Illustration 22. Tying up the treadles. Treadle 1 has been tied to lamms 1 and 2. Treadle 2 has been tied to lamms 2 and 3. This is in accordance with the Worst tie-up. Snitch knots are used to tie the cords coming from the lamms to those coming from the treadles. Lamm 4 is not shown.

These tie-ups are for the four-harness loom which has a sinking shed (page 14). A *shed* is the opening made in the warp when the treadles are operated. If your loom is one that has a rising shed (page 15), you can still use either system of tying up the treadles with this difference: In place of using the x's as guides for the tie-up, use the blank spaces. In other words, Diagram 3 would have treadle 1 tied to lamms 3 and 4 instead of 1 and 2, etc.

Floor looms with four treadles instead of six are tied up with the direct tie-up as given below:

When the direct tie-up is used, it is necessary to use two treadles at a time to accomplish the work that one treadle can do in the other two tie-ups. For instance, in the Worst tie-up treadle number 6 is tied up to harnesses 1 and 4. To use these same harnesses with the direct tie-up, you will have to use treadle number 1 and treadle number 4 together. This requires the use of two feet at the same time, but if one is agile, one foot can straddle two treadles if they are adjacent as in the case of treadles 1 and 2, for instance. This produces a rather rolling motion of the hips which may be its greatest advan-

DIRECT TIE-UP

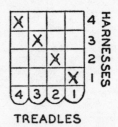

TREADLES
(FRONT OF LOOM)
Diagram 5.

tage! On the other hand, it is sometimes necessary to make use of three harnesses simultaneously, and this is more easily done with the direct tie-up. It is also possible with the direct tie-up to operate the harnesses one by one.

All cords used for tie-up purposes on a loom must be non-stretching and very strong. Loom and weaving supply houses handle cord for this purpose. If you do not have ready access to such supply houses or in an emergency, buy a hank of what is called "mason line" from a hardware store. This braided cord, while a little stiff at first, will do very well. Upholsterer's cord can also be used.

Table looms, being without treadles, have no tie-ups and the harnesses are operated by means of hand levers. For an explanation of how to change the treadling directions given for a floor loom into those for a table loom or other rising shed loom, see Chapters 9 and 10.

Chapter 8

PUTTING IN A HEADING AND "TROUBLE SHOOTING"

Large wedge-shaped spaces will be seen between the groups of warp ends where they are laced in front. To make these disappear, several rows of plain weave are woven, using alternately treadles 3 and 4 of the Worst tie-up, Diagram 4 of the previous chapter, and very heavy material for weft. This is known as *putting in a heading*.

First, adjust the tension of the warp. There is on every loom a foot or hand lever or other means of adjustment which moves the warp forward and also a ratchet with a catch or dog, or a brake of some sort which holds the warp in place at the tension desired for weaving. (See Illustration 24.) The warp should be fairly taut but not to the extent that the harnesses will be hindered in their operation. On the other hand, it is impossible to weave if the warp is too slack. It will be necessary for you to experiment to arrive at the tension which seems best for good work for you.

To put in a heading, take some very heavy material—rag strips, rope or anything else that comes to hand. It can be pushed with the hands through the opening called a shed which you make in the warp by stepping on treadle number 3 (the Worst tie-up is used from now on) and by holding it down with your foot. Or you can wind this weft on a flat (stick) shuttle. It is not necessary to fasten in the weft at the selvages in this operation. Weft, you will remember is the name given to any of the threads which cross and interweave with the warp.

If you are using a table loom, pull down levers 1 and 3 together for your first row of weaving.

Bring the beater against this row of weft, thus beating it in place. Step on treadle number 4, or pull down levers 2 and 4, releasing treadle number 3 or hand levers 1 and 3, and put in another row of the coarse weft. Beat this row in place. The weft can be in lengths long enough to go through the shed and hang down at the selvages for a few inches, or it can be a continuous piece. Continue to use treadles 3 and 4 alternately this way until the wedges disappear. As you do so, watch carefully to see that no mistakes have been made in your setting-up process, for this is the time to remedy them.

CORRECTING ERRORS

Improper Sleying

If, for instance, you have made a mistake in the sleying of the reed in spite of all your precautions, either by crowding too many warp ends in one dent or by skipping dents, there is nothing to do but to take out the heading, the lacing cord, and the knots and remove the warp out of the reed to the nearest selvage and then to re-sley it. So scan the top of your *tabby sheds* closely. If you see a place where there is a space wider than the rest, you have skipped a dent. If you see a place where there are two or more warp ends coming from one dent when the shed is opened, you have probably crowded the warp ends there. Crowded or skipped dents will make streaks in your material which no amount of beating or laundering will hide.

Crossed-over Warp Ends

A warp end which does not rise or fall as the treadles are used but remains in the center of the shed in front of the reed has been crossed from the heddle over to the wrong dent. This is easily remedied once the offender has been found. There are two warp ends involved, in fact, one crossed over the other. Break them off at the knot, add on a short length of warp to each one, put them through their correct dents, and then tie them around the lacing cord at the knot in any way, just so that the tension is the same as the others.

Misthreading of Draft

Mistakes in threading are more unfortunate but should not be too serious since you have checked your threading carefully as you went along. Sometimes, however, a warp end which should be on harness 3, for instance, is found to be on harness 2. This forms in the shed what is called a *flat,* that is, two warp ends side by side rise or fall together in the shed when plain weave is treadled on treadles 3 and 4, so that the weaving is imperfect.

To repair a flat, take the warp end out of the wrong harness, having first cut it at the knot. Then with a piece of carpet warp or other strong thread more than twice as long as your heddles, tie a string heddle on the correct harnesses and in the correct place. Rethread the warp end through this string heddle, re-sley it in the reed, tie on a short bit of warp yarn to make it long enough, and with a pin anchor it as shown in Illustration 23.

To tie a string heddle, first make what is called a *doup* by centering this piece of heddle cord under the bar of the harness where the string heddle is to be tied. Tie a square knot with the two ends so that the knot comes in line with the lower part of all the eyes of the other heddles. Tie another square knot above this one on a level with the top of all the eyes of the heddles, thus making an eye in the string heddle. (See square knot, Illustration 20, page

73.) Then tie the ends on top of the heddle bar at the upper part of the harness using another square knot. This tie should not bind the string heddle to the bars of the harness, for it must be able to slip along them as the other heddles do. Thread the warp end through the eye of the string heddle. The unwanted steel heddle remains in the harness for it will not interfere with the weaving in any way. Weaving supply houses stock snap-on repair heddles which are very useful in such cases for they obviate the necessity of tying on a string heddle.

Omission of a Threading

Suppose you find that you have completely left out one thread of the draft. This also causes a flat to occur in one of your tabby sheds. Don't pull out the entire threading! Wind some of the warp yarn on a spool or on one of the bobbins which fit into your boat shuttles and use this to take the place of the warp end which was omitted, tying in a string heddle for it on the correct harness, or using a repair heddle. Now, of course, you will have to re-sley the warp to the nearest selvage to accommodate this extra warp end after which it is anchored in front with a pin. In addition, you will need to add weights (metal washers or dress weights are good) to the bobbin hanging down over the slabstock until you have it at the same tension as the others. This can be ascertained once you begin to weave for if the warp end looks puckery in the cloth, it is not weighted enough; too tightly drawn, and it needs less weight. Weighted warp ends hanging down behind the slabstock may look untidy, but they work and that is the main thing. (See Illustration 23.)

Now is the time also to adjust the length of the treadle and harness cords up or down, until the lower part of the open shed just comes in contact with the lower edge of the reed in the beater. This permits free clearance for your shuttle to pass through the shed. On a counterbalanced loom the harnesses and the reed should be at such a height that when a warp end comes from the slabstock,

through the eye of a heddle, into a dent of the reed and thence over the breast beam in front, it is horizontal, parallel to the floor. On a loom with a rising shed, however, you will note that the manufacturer has adjusted the harnesses so that the warp is about one inch lower at the heddle eyes on the smaller looms and two to three inches lower on the larger looms, than it is at slabstock and breast beam. Better sheds are obtained on these looms when this is so. (See also Chapter 10, Adjustment of the Harnesses.)

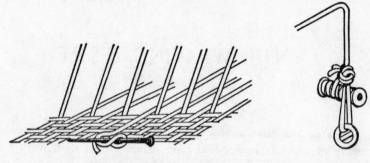

Illustration 23. The forgotten warp end.

Chapter 9

THE WEAVING ITSELF

You are now almost ready to weave, though it still is necessary to wind some *bobbins*, also called *quills*, with weft. For your weft you can use, if you like, the same thread as was used for the warp, though in that case it will be called weft. On page 107, you will find a discussion of bobbin winders which are a necessary part of a weaver's equipment. (See Illustration 31.)

WINDING A BOBBIN

Let us suppose that you are using a paper quill which is a tube about the diameter of a lead pencil and about 3¼ inches long. Place the quill on the tapered shank of your winder, and tie the end of the weft to it with the beginning of a surgeon's knot (Illustration 20, page 73). This, as seen from the sketch, is only the well known overhand knot with the free end of it tucked in again. It holds the weft in place once the winding begins and is easily released when the bobbin is empty. Or you can merely wind the weft a few times around the quill to hold it in place. Put your weft in a can or other suitable container on the floor under the winder so that it cannot roll all over the place while you are winding.

Weft must be wound on a bobbin so that a little mound about a quarter of an inch from the left of the bobbin is formed, taking great care the while that the thread does not wind beyond this mound and out towards the left end. When a mound has been wound at one side, shift to the other and wind in similar fashion. Then fill in the center. A well wound bobbin feels hard and firm and is about three-quarters of an inch in diameter. It is a mistake to fill bobbins too full.

Just as surely as you allow the weft in winding to fall off the mound towards the outside end of the quill, you are going to have trouble. The weft then will start to slide off the quill and when it is placed in the boat shuttle will wind around its shank. This will stop the smooth progress of the shuttle as it is thrown through the shed. A bobbin of linen weft is particularly hard for a beginner to wind because linen is so wiry. Indeed, linen must be held in the fingers with so much tension while the bobbin is being wound that it almost burns them, and even so linen tends to fall off the ends of a bobbin.

Some shuttles are provided with spool-like bobbins. On them the winding should start at one end and take the form of a cone with the tapered end towards the center. Then wind the other end of the spool in like manner, leaving a depression in the middle which is not filled in until the last.

Unless a bobbin is properly wound, you cannot expect to do good weaving. It is, therefore, very important that you practice winding bobbins until you can produce one that has all the characteristics mentioned above.

BEGINNING TO WEAVE

From all that has gone before, you can see readily that a weaver does most of the hard work before sitting down at the loom to weave. Now for the fun of weaving!

First, it will be necessary and very important that you as a beginner practice plain weave, or *tabby*. By means of the long-handled or long-pedalled catch on the rear ratchet, release the tension on your warp and bring some of it forward by pumping up and down with the handle of the front catch. Recall what was said regarding the proper tension at which the warp should be kept for weaving.

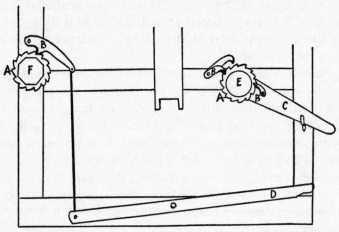

Illustration 24. The warp on a loom may be moved forward as weaving progresses by this mechanism; the ratchets with their dogs are for maintaining the tension. See also (O) on the frontispiece. A. Front and rear ratchets. B. Dogs. C. Hand lever for releasing tension on cloth beam and also for use in moving the warp forward. D. Pedal to release tension on the warp beam. A loom equipped with a friction brake does not have the rear ratchet but substitutes a steel wire wound several times around the warp beam.

Do not move so much warp forward that the reed in the beater will not be able to touch the last row of your heading. Indeed, you should form the habit of moving the warp forward frequently while weaving and of weaving only within about a three or four inch space, thus keeping the angle at which the beater strikes the last row of the weaving more constant.

Place the bobbin you have wound into one of the boat shuttles so that the weft comes from under the bobbin and out through the hole or slot in the side of the shuttle. Hold the shuttle in your right hand with this hole or slot towards you and the flat side of the shuttle towards the reed. (See Illustration 25.)

Depress treadle number 3 (Worst tie-up) with your right foot,

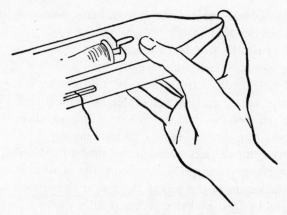

Illustration 25. How the boat shuttle is held.

holding open the shed and throw the shuttle from right to left through it in front of the reed. Fasten the end of the weft as shown in Illustration 26. See how the harnesses tied to this treadle are lowered (counterbalanced or sinking shed loom) or raised (jack type or table loom). On a table loom use hand levers numbers 1 and 3 both together. Hand levers are numbered from front to back. Catch the shuttle with the left hand, holding it in the same way as before.

Illustration 26. Beginning the weft. Holding open the shed with treadle 3, the end of the weft is placed on top of the first warp end of the upper part of the shed and then down into the same shed again for a short distance. Sketch shows the weft being put through for the next row on treadle 4.

It should never be necessary to reach in after it, for the impetus given the shuttle should be just enough to send it flying through the shed. This comes with practice. Grasp the beater in the center of the top (D in the frontispiece) with the right hand and give a sharp beat to the row of weft—a beat, not just a squeeze. The nature of the beat differs with various fibers, wool being beaten lightly; linen is given a heavier beat.

Change to treadle number 4 (hand levers 2 and 4 pulled down on a table loom). Treadle number 4 is used with the left foot and while still holding down the treadle, beat once more using the right hand on the beater and in the center as before. Now the upper and lower parts of the shed have changed places; those warp ends which were on top before are now on the bottom.

Throw the shuttle back through the shed to the right, catching it with the right hand. Beat this second row of weft using the left hand on the center of the top of the beater (handtree). Change to the other tabby shed by using either treadle number 3 or levers 1 and 3 together as the case may be and beat again. Throw the shuttle through this open shed back to the left again to be caught with the left hand. Continue in this way until an even rhythm has been established, saying to yourself as you do so: *throw, catch, beat, change, beat; throw, catch, beat, change, beat* . . . over and over again.

Notice that in throwing the shuttle and treadling the loom you are using your left hand and left foot together and your right hand and right foot together. Treadle by sense of touch, and do not bend down to look at your feet. It is an excellent idea to wear low-heeled shoes or only socks when treadling a loom.

For those of you who have sectional beams or are using ready-spooled warp, lease sticks can now be inserted in the warp. While they are not essential to the weaving they will keep the warp ends in perfect order should you wish at any time to change the threading of this warp to another draft. To insert lease sticks, open one of the tabby sheds and push a lease stick through the shed which is formed *behind* the harnesses. Move this stick to the rear of the loom. Open the other tabby shed, insert another lease stick, also behind the harnesses and move this stick to the rear. Tie the ends of these sticks together and then tie them loosely to the slabstock. You will see that the warp ends are now going over and under the lease sticks one by one thus keeping them in perfect threading order.

Avoiding Draw-in

To prevent the material you are weaving from narrowing or drawing-in at the selvages, the weft should be left loose in the shed just before beating it and placed in the shed at an angle as shown in Illustration 27. If this is not done, the strain of drawing-in becomes so great that the selvage threads break and the reed may be damaged. Drawing-in occurs because the weft in the shed is crimped by the interweaving which takes place between warp and

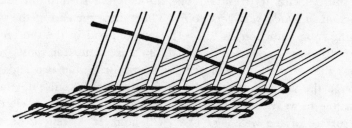

Illustration 27. Angle of insertion of the weft thread.

weft and which shortens the latter, causing the material to become narrower than the width of the warp in the reed. No amount of fussing or pulling at the selvages will cause them to become wider, once they are drawn in, so form the habit of placing the weft in the shed at an angle and do not pull on the weft with the hand that holds the shuttle. Some draw-in is bound to occur, but strive to keep it down to a minimum.

The beater must be grasped in the center because if not, your rows of weft will not lie parallel to the breast beam but will climb uphill at one side or the other.

Good Selvages

At first your selvages will appear as if mice had been gnawing at them and often it happens that one selvage looks better than the other. There is, indeed, no royal road to good selvages, for they come with practice and experience. There are, however, some ex-

cellent hints about the winding of bobbins and the making of good
selvages given in the article entitled "Your Selvage is Showing,"
written by Bill Carter which appeared in Volume 3, No. 1 of the
Handweaver & Craftsman. The Shuttle Craft Guild Bulletin for
August 1948 has some excellent suggestions. (See Bibliography.)

FASTENING THE WEFT

When weft in the bobbin runs out, never tie on the new to the
old. Simply keep the shed open in which you were weaving. Insert
the shuttle with its fresh bobbin through the shed *in the same
direction in which you were going.* Then allow the end of the weft
coming from your bobbin to overlap the old end in the shed for a
short distance. A quarter to a half inch is plenty for most wefts
unless the warp ends are sleyed far apart. Bring the two ends up
through the warp on top of the shed and let them stick up there.
Continue to weave for an inch or so, then cut the ends off close to
the surface of the weaving. They will hold. It is well to do this
piecing near one selvage or the other where it is away from the
center of interest. (See Illustration 28.) A knot in weft is cut out and
treated the same way, never woven in.

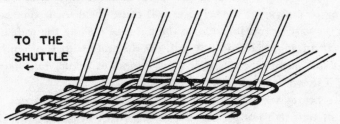

TO THE SHUTTLE

Illustration 28.   The new weft being added is the same as the one that was
being used. If an entirely different weft is to be used next, the last row should
be finished off as shown in Illustration 29. The new weft is then fastened in the
next shed at the same side as the old weft was fastened off.

Very heavy wefts should be frayed out at the ends so that where
they overlap at the join they are not too bulky. When starting to
weave with a heavy rug filler for instance, separate the end coming
from your shuttle into its separate strands for about four inches.

Eliminate one of these strands by pulling it until it frays off. Now when the remaining strands are run back into the shed as shown on the sketch, the resultant overlapping will not be too noticeable. Do this same thing at the end of the piece of weaving. When your shuttle runs out and you wish to continue with the same weft, separate the strands, fray out and discard one strand from both the old and the new weft so that where they overlap in the shed the join will be neatly made.

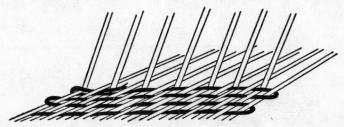

Illustration 29.   Fastening the weft at the end of the weaving, or when making a change in the nature or color of the weft.

To fasten in the weft at the end of the weaving, do not leave it dangling from the selvage. Instead, after you have thrown the shuttle for your last row, keep your foot on the treadle, thus holding open the shed. Cut the weft and bring it around the outside selvage warp end. Next, bring the weft back into the shed for about a half inch and put it up through the warp on the upper part of the shed. (See Illustration 29.) This is also the way to finish off a bobbin when you wish to change to another color.

BROKEN WARP ENDS

When a warp end breaks—alas, they do break now and then—it is not hard to mend it. First, measure off a length of warp yarn long enough to reach from the breast beam to the slabstock with some extra for tying. Working from the front, put the new length of warp through the space left vacant in the reed when the old warp end broke. If you have sleyed the reed two ends to a dent as described in Chapter 6, then find the dent where one of the pair of warp ends is missing and put this new warp end through it from the front of the reed. Pull this new warp end almost completely through the reed and then take the short end and anchor it around a pin placed in the woven material directly under the break. (See Illustration 30.)

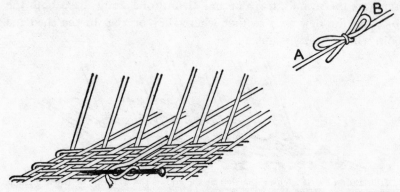

Illustration 30. Replacing a broken warp end. A is the new warp end. B is the old broken warp end.

Thread the long end of this warp end through the heddle which you find either to be empty or still holding the broken original warp end (which should be taken out of the heddle). Draw the new warp end to the rear of the loom and tie it to the original warp end at or near the slabstock. Use a bowknot, keeping the tension of this substitute warp end the same as all the others. During the weaving from here on watch this bowknot to see that it does not interfere with the making of a good shed by getting tangled up in the warp. Untie it frequently and retie it back at the slabstock.

The broken end of the original warp thread in front of the reed is wound around the pin with the new warp end, that is, if it is long enough.

Continue to weave to the end of your piece or until you can undo the bowknot and bring the original warp end coming up from the warp beam back to the front by threading it through its heddle and dent in the reed. The warp end which you substituted can then be pulled through to the front of the reed and clipped off leaving, however, enough to thread on a needle later. Anchor the original warp end on a pin in front, and test it with your fingers to see that it is at the correct tension. Later, the old warp end and the new must be darned back in for a short distance by means of a needle, or else there will be a weak spot in the material. When this is done, the two ends can be clipped short.

WHAT WENT WRONG?

To weave well in tabby is the test of a good weaver. Watch your work carefully. Are there streaks across the width of the warp every once in a while? You are probably not beating evenly or perhaps you are not being careful to adjust the tension at the dog and ratchet so that it feels the same every time you move the warp forward. If there are loops left by the weft at the selvages, you are not pulling on the weft enough, or perhaps you have it placed in the shed at too much of an angle.

If you find that you are drawing the warp in too much, start over by putting in a few rows of coarse weft to spread the warp out again. Carpet warp used for weft is good for a beginner to practice on. Strive for good rhythm in weaving (*throw, catch, beat, change, beat*). If you find that your rows of weft persist in running uphill at the selvages, you have tied the outside bunches of your warp too loosely to the apron stick in front. On the other hand, if your weft turns down at the selvages, these outer warp ends have been tied too tightly to the apron stick. Selvages are meant to be drawn in a *little* closer together than the balance of the weaving so do not have them too open. You can see the reason for the statement that there is no royal road to good selvages!

WEAVING WITH TWO SHUTTLES

To weave the Rose Path draft which you have threaded (Chapter 6), you will use other sheds than just the two for tabby and you will need to use another boat shuttle in addition to the one you have been using. Thread this second shuttle with a bobbin wound with a coarser weft than 20/2, such as crochet cotton, 6-strand floss, carpet warp or wool, for instance, and in color. Call this shuttle *B*. The other shuttle carries a finer weft, 20/2 cotton, for instance, in natural to match the warp. This is shuttle *A*. Before and after each row of the pattern weft (colored) there is thrown a row in tabby or plain weave using shuttle A. These tabby or *binder rows,* as they are called, are not written down in directions given for weaving because a weaver understands that they are to be woven. However, for the sake of the beginners, let us note down the complete treadling directions for Rose Path, using only one of its many, many treadling possibilities. These directions are for the sinking shed loom and the Worst tie-up.

Rising shed floor looms make use of the same directions but you must remember to have your treadles tied to the blanks of the tie-up.

Begin with treadle 3	with	Shuttle A	thrown from the right
Follow with " 1	"	" B	" " " "
" 4	"	" A	" " " left
" 2	"	" B	" " " "
" 3	"	" A	" " " right
" 5	"	" B	" " " "
" 4	"	" A	" " " left
" 6	"	" B	" " " "
" 3	"	" A	" " " right
" 6	"	" B	" " " "
" 4	"	" A	" " " left
" 5	"	" B	" " " "
" 3	"	" A	" " " right
" 2	"	" B	" " " "
" 4	"	" A	" " " left
" 1	"	" B	" " " "

And begin again from the beginning, repeating over and over this little variation for an all-over pattern. Notice that both shuttles are started from the right, the ends of the wefts fastened as shown in Illustration 26. Note, also, that the treadles used for the binder rows with shuttle A alternate.....3, 4, 3, 4, etc., and that when you are using treadle 3 the shuttle is always thrown from the right and when you are using treadle 4, the shuttle is thrown from the left. The treadlings used with the other shuttle, however, may find it either at the left or at the right. This is true of all two-shuttle weaving.

If you are already a weaver, the only directions you will need for this are those for shuttle B as follows: Treadles 1, 2, 5 once each. Treadle 6 twice. Treadles 5, 2 and 1 once each and repeat from the beginning.

Table looms have rising sheds but no treadles so substitute for these directions as follows:

For treadle 1 use levers 3 and 4 together (pulled down)
"   "   2 "   "   1 and 4   "   "   "
"   "   3 "   "   2 and 4   "   "   "...this is one tabby shed
"   "   4 "   "   1 and 3   "   "   "...this is the other
"   "   5 "   "   1 and 2   "   "   "
"   "   6 "   "   2 and 3   "   "   "

Refer to the Worst tie-up, page 78, and you will see that the levers used for the table loom which correspond to treadle 1 for instance are the same as the numbers of the lamms which would be tied to the *blanks* of the tie-up, i.e., 3 and 4. This is because the table loom has a rising shed. The above conversion table holds true of any directions given for a sinking shed loom which you wish to change over for the rising shed looms. It is true that you can use the regular counter-balanced or sinking shed treadling directions on these looms without any change-over, but the material will be woven wrong side up.

Variations on the Rose Path pattern come as a result of experiment. You can treadle in any order you wish. You can repeat a treadling as many times as you wish and the binder rows used with shuttle A will hold them in place. You can introduce different colors in the weft (and in the warp when it was planned, of course). You can weave without any binder rows at all, but in this case you cannot repeat a treadling twice in succession unless you catch the shuttle around the outside warp end for, unless you do, the second row will pull right out again. You can vary the texture by the use of dull and glossy fibers, bumpy and smooth fibers, etc. Try using a coarse white or natural weft for the pattern rows with shuttle B and put colored 20/2 in the other shuttle for the tabby rows. A sampler made on the Rose Path treadling is a most satisfying project, as has been demonstrated by Berta Frey in *Seven Projects in Rose Path*. See bibliography.

Rose Path was chosen for this threading only as an example of a small, easily understood and easily threaded draft. It is not within the scope of this book to enter into a discussion of pattern drafts. The bibliography has a list of many fine texts in which they may be found.

RULES OF THE DAY

Before you leave your weaving for the day, it is a good habit to ease the tension on your warp just a little. If you are using a cotton warp and live in a damp climate, you will be very wise, indeed, to do this because cotton tightens up considerably in dampness. A half dozen or more warp ends have been known to snap during the night just on this account.

Now is also the time to insist that nothing be placed on the warp of your loom and, of course, to put nothing on it yourself, not even your shuttle for any length of time. Why it is that people seem to think warps are good places to lay books, coats, hats, etc., I do not know, but I do know that you must be firm on this subject, and get the family started off right from the very beginning. A warp that has sagging places in it because things have been laid on it is very sad indeed.

Chapter 10

A FEW POINTERS

At the risk of seeming repetitious, let me recapitulate a few things before you are left to your own weaving devices.

ADJUSTMENT OF THE HARNESSES

Theoretically, the harnesses of a counterbalanced loom should be hung so that after being threaded, sleyed, and tied, the warp will come through the reed about one-third of the distance up from the bottom of it. But there is nothing more annoying to a weaver than to have the bottom of a shed so ragged that the shuttle catches in the warp ends there. For this reason in actual practice, the height of the warp in the reed should be adjusted until, when the sheds are open, the lower part rests on the bottom of the reed. This is brought about by adjusting the length of the various cords used to tie up the harnesses, lamms, and treadles. The use of snitch knots makes this easy to do. If the construction of your loom permits, the reed may be raised or lowered in the beater until the bottom warp ends in the sheds just touch the bottom of the reed. You must, however, watch to see that the warp is still in a straight line from the breast beam to the slabstock or the two sides of the material will differ, the warp predominating on one side, the weft on the other. But, as a rule, if the loom is a good one, you can have the warp at the bottom of the reed when a shed is open, and still have it in a straight line when the shed is closed. Although this does increase the friction on the warp ends, it is desirable to have the warp this way for reasons stated above.

I do not advise that you change the cords, etc., of table looms and other rising shed looms for they have left the factory in working order and are much too complicated for a novice to adjust.

REEDS AND THEIR CARE

Why is a reed called a reed? In olden times reeds were just what their name indicates—actually made with flat reed strips for partitions and with twine wound between them to keep them spaced apart. Naturally, these old reeds were not as accurately made as the ones we have today.

Reeds vary in size for home use from 4 to 40 dents to the inch. The size of each reed is usually stamped upon it. Those most commonly owned by handweavers are the 15, 12 and 10 dent reeds. It is better to use these coarser reeds and put several warp ends through each dent for the finer materials, rather than to use fine reeds since the more partitions a reed has, the more friction there will be on the warp ends. In addition, should you ever wish to tie on a new warp to an old one (thus saving yourself the task of rethreading the draft), you will quickly see the advantage of using a coarser reed when the knots slip through the dents so easily. Then, too, some of us find that our eyes are not as good as they used to be! Ridges which sometimes are noted in the woven material as a result of sleying several warp ends in a dent disappear in laundering.

When you buy a reed, get a long one and then cut it into the length desired with a hack saw for then you can have two reeds for just a little more than the price of one. While a standard reed is 4½ inches high, most beaters are adjustable to accommodate higher ones. Because new reeds are covered with an oily film, you must clean them well before use. A carbon tetrachloride spot remover, which you can get at drugstores and hardware stores, cleans them readily.

If a reed is very badly rusted, there is nothing much that can be done for it. The use of steel wool and plenty of "elbow grease" will usually take care of slightly rusted ones. If you find that your reeds are rusting, it will pay you to buy stainless steel ones.

One method of determining how many ends of warp to put in each inch of a reed is to wind some of the warp around a ruler, covering in this manner an inch space without crowding the warp thread. Count the number of times it was necessary to wind in order to fill the inch space, and then use less than this figure—the mill practice is to use about half the number. Of course, there are excellent thread charts to be had which will also give you these figures. See page 167 of the bibliography.

Many weaving books are published in foreign languages, especially Swedish, and in them directions for sleying the reed are given in the metric system, a common one being "88 per 10 cm." Ten centimeters is about four inches, so this would call for a reed with 22 dents per inch. In this country a 12-dent reed is more available so use this instead, placing two warp ends in each dent. Two extra dents per inch will not usually make too great a difference.

If a reed is not to be used for some length of time, it should be put away in a dry place. Lay it flat to prevent it from warping out of shape. When the storage is to be for a long time, a light coating of machine oil or kerosene will keep it free from rust. There are also sprays to prevent rusting of reeds.

Versatility of a 15-Dent Reed

A 15-dent reed is a good all-around size to have for it comes in handy for many articles of weaving. The following table, prepared by Rupert Peters, head of the Weaving Department at the Penland School of Handicrafts in Penland, North Carolina, shows what can be done with it.

1st dent	2nd dent	3rd dent	Results in	Application
1 end	skip	1 end	7½ ends per in.	Rag rugs (8 to 12 per inch are preferable, however)
1 end	1 end	1 end	15 ends per in.	For use with carpet warp or coarse crochet cottons; use for knitting bags, mats with rug filler for weft, etc.
1 end	2 ends	1 end	22½ ends per in.	Medium weight sports jackets with worsted for warp (15/2), etc.
2 ends	2 ends	2 ends	30 ends per in.	The most common sleying; 20/2 cotton and 40/2 linen warps, dress materials, table linens, etc.
3 ends	3 ends	3 ends	45 ends per in.	50/2 linen warp yarn for fine materials and also for fine cotton warp yarns.
4 ends	4 ends	4 ends	60 ends per in.	Very fine yarns.

THE WARP PLAN

While many times a weaver winds on a warp of a certain yardage and keeps on weaving until it is used up, there are at other times special projects which require closer figuring. How is this done?

Let us suppose that you wish to weave a luncheon set consisting of eight place mats and eight napkins, all to be woven on the same warp, with the mats 12 × 18 inches finished and the napkins 12 × 12 inches. Start off by figuring as follows:

8 place mats, each 18 inches long will require	144	inches
8 napkins, each 12 inches long will require	96	"
32 hems for the above, 1 inch each "	32	"
Total	272	"

But if you wind only this amount of warp, you will never have enough to weave this set because there will be shrinkage both in the weaving and the laundering. Always remember to take into consideration that the amount of woven material is less than the warp wound. Just how much less varies so much with the yarns, beat, tension at which the warp is kept during the weaving, sett in the reed (that is, how many ends per inch), the weave you are using, and the finishing (laundering, etc.,) that only experience will tell you how much to allow. Realizing all this, better count on an average amount of shrinkage which for cotton warp is 10% and for linen would be 15%.

In addition to this, there should be an allowance for tying the warp to the cloth beam in front at the apron stick and for the fact that there is always quite a bit of warp between the harnesses and the slabstock which at the very end of a warp cannot be woven. A yard more warp will take care of these two items very generously.

Then there is need for extra warp length to take care of your experiments and to enable you to adjust the beating correctly. Adding these things we have:

For the set itself	272	inches
10% for shrinkage (cotton warp)	27	"
Tying in and waste in rear	36	"
Experiments, etc., about	18	"
Grand total	353	" or about 10 yards of warp to prepare

Now, how wide will you need to make this warp? The mats and napkins are to be 12 inches wide, finished, but this does not mean 12 inches wide in the reed, for there is draw-in to be considered as you already know. Just how much to allow for draw-in varies, for in addition to the factors already mentioned above in connection with the shrinkage in length which apply here also, there is also the personal equation to be considered because some weavers habitually draw in the width of woven material more than others. An inch allowance will be about right until you learn to control your draw-in. This is largely a matter of establishing good rhythm in weaving as was described in the last chapter.

With regard to handwoven yard goods, there is usually allowed three inches per yard of width for draw-in, so that a 36-inch material in the reed will produce usually not more and sometimes less than 33 inches finished. This reference to finishing of yardages does not mean merely the hand laundering which you give to the material but refers to the commercial process known as *finishing* whereby worsted and woolen materials are thickened or *fulled* before they are fit to be made into garments. Oftentimes this finishing process is partly done by the weavers themselves by washing the goods with mild soaps, after which they are dry cleaned. For excellent accounts of the weaving and finishing of handwoven wool and worsted yardages, see Roger Millen's book *Weave Your Own Tweeds,* and the Shuttle Craft Guild Bulletins for November and December 1952. Both sources are mentioned in the bibliography.

This matter of the finishing of handwoven yardages is a very important one, because good weaving can be ruined by poor finishing. Inasmuch as the shrinkage can be considerable, it is always wise to take the time and trouble to make a short sample warp, about 18 inches wide, weave it and finish it or have it finished to ascertain how the material is going to look and whether it is suitable for your purpose.

Returning to the subject at hand, to weave this luncheon set you have found out that you will need to prepare a warp ten yards long and thirteen inches wide in the reed. How much warp yarn should you, therefore, order? If the material is to have, let us say, 30 warp ends for each inch of width of the goods (a frequent calculation for finer table linens), you will need 30×13 or 390 warp ends in all. Each end will be ten yards long so you must have at least 3900 yards of warp yarn at hand.

If you decide to use a linen warp, choose a 2-ply warp yarn known as 40/2. This has 6000 yards per pound. Or, if you choose cotton, a 20/2 cotton warp yarn which has 8400 yards to the pound can be used. You will find on the sample cards which you receive from supply houses that the yardage per pound of the various yarns is stated. Both the 40/2 linen and the 20/2 cotton are fine yarns and usually set at 30 warp ends per inch in the reed.

How much weft will you need? If your luncheon set is to be woven in a linen weave such as those known as "M's and O's" or a "Bronson," then in each inch that you weave of the warp there should be thirty rows (also called picks or shots) of weaving and you would have to adjust your beating accordingly. This is what is known as *square count* (because there are as many rows of weft per inch as there are warp ends per inch), and the amount of weft needed would be about the same as that required for the warp. The reference above to various weaves will become clear to you as you follow the explanation given in the second part of this book.

If you choose a linen thread for weft (and sometimes linen weft is used on cotton warp yarn), buy the single-ply linen of the corresponding size of your warp. This is because a single-ply linen is much less expensive than the plied linens and is softer, less wiry, so that it beats in better. A size 20/1 linen weft is the equivalent in *grist* (size) of a 40/2 linen warp yarn and can also be used on a 20/2 cotton warp. Size 16/1 linen weft, which is just a little coarser, also works in well.

If you are not intending to use a linen weave, such as those mentioned above, but wish to weave in an allover pattern using color and a draft such as Rose Path, for instance, the best rule to follow is: Buy plenty—dye lots differ! For pattern weaving it is usual to use two wefts, as you already know, the finer for the tabby shots and a coarser, colored one for the pattern as was explained in the last chapter. The tabby rows are often woven using the same thread as the warp while the pattern rows may be woven with a number of different wefts including six-strand floss, crochet cotton, carpet warp, and wool. Linen as a weft for pattern weaving does not beat in well so it is not generally used.

When you measure the length of your place mats and napkins on the loom as you are weaving, remember to allow that extra 10 per cent or 15 per cent to the overall length of the piece. In other words, place mats on a 20/2 cotton warp which are planned to be 18 inches long plus two inches for hems must be woven not 20 inches long but 22 inches long. It is better, also, to make your measurements with the tension off the warp.

Thread Sizes, Yardages per Pound, Etc.

Many weavers are puzzled about the yardage they may expect to find in each pound of the yarns they are using and also about what the different numbers mean on the labels, so perhaps a discussion of these items will not be amiss here.

Cotton and linen yarn, both in the warp and the weft yarns, are designated by numbers to show their grist, that is, their size. They may be purchased as single-ply or they may be plied, so we have 2-ply, 3-ply, 4-ply, etc., yarns. Speaking of identical fibers of the same ply, the higher the number, the finer the thread. A 20/2 in linen or cotton is, therefore, finer than a 10/2. At the mill, these fibers are spun so that there is a definite and known number of yards per pound. To spin a 2-ply yarn from a single-ply yarn the length, that is, the yardage of the fiber per pound, is doubled upon itself and the two strands are then plied or twisted together in the spinning. Therefore, you can see that a 20/2 yarn, for instance, will have but one-half the number of yards in each pound that the 20/1 fiber has.

Given the size of the yarn or, as we say, *the count* and knowing the ply, you can by the use of a simple formula arrive at the yardage per pound. For cotton the formula is based upon the fact that a pound of No. 1 single-ply (1/1) yarn contains 840 yards. Therefore:

$$\text{Yardage per pound} = \frac{\text{Count} \times 840}{\text{the ply}}$$

Solving for 20/2 cotton yarn, you have:

$$\text{Yardage per pound} = \frac{20 \times 840}{2} \text{ or } 8400 \text{ yards}$$

For linen the formula is as follows. It is based on the fact that a single-ply No. 1 linen yarn contains 300 yards per pound. This amount is known as a *lea*.

$$\text{Yardage per pound} = \frac{\text{Count} \times 300}{\text{ply}}$$

Solving for 40/2 linen, you have:

$$\text{Yardage per pound} = \frac{40 \times 300}{2} \text{ or } 6000 \text{ yards per pound}$$

Woolen and Worsted Yarns

The situation with regard to these yarns is complicated. Zielinski's *Encyclopedia* (see Bibliography) lists seven different systems in use in determining the count and yardages per pound. In the United States, however, the most frequent terms encountered with regard to woolen yarns are *cuts* and *runs*. A cut of No. 1 single-ply woolen yarn measures 300 yards and weighs one pound. The term *run* is used in another system. A run of No. 1 single-ply woolen yarn weighs one pound and measures 1600 yards.

Worsted is a hard-twisted, smooth-surfaced yarn spun from long-stapled pure wool and is so combed that its fibers lie parallel to each other. The term may also apply to a similarly spun mixed yarn. The unit used with reference to this yarn is called a *count*. Each count of single-ply worsted yarn measures 560 yards and the number of the yarn depends upon how many counts of single-ply yarn there are in a pound.

Silk, rayon, and the newer fibers of nylon, dacron and orlon are finding favor with many handweavers nowadays. In order to eliminate all the confusion concerning the various systems in use of numbering these different yarns, a handweaver would do well to buy yarns direct from concerns which cater to handweavers because they mark the yardages and sizes of their products. But if you wish to go further into the matter, I would refer you to Marguerite Davison's *A Handweaver's Pattern Book,* especially in the revised edition and Harriette J. Brown's *Hand Weaving for Pleasure and Profit.* Both of these treat the subject in considerable detail.

ACCESSORIES

Bobbins and Bobbin Winders

There are good bobbin winders on the market, both manual and electric but various homemade substitutes have been devised. The shaft of one of her electric mixer attachments has been in use by one weaver of my acquaintance for many years just for this pur-

pose. Another has rigged up a winder by using the bobbin winder
of the sewing machine. If you wish to have an electric winder made,
use a motor of about 1600 to 2200 R. P. M. (revolutions per minute)
such as an old sewing machine motor and have a machine shop fit a
tapered spindle on it so that your bobbins or spools will fit. (Illustration 31.)

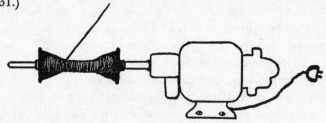

Illustration 31. A bobbin winder.

About three-quarters of an inch diameter is sufficient to wind a
paper bobbin for it is a mistake to wind them too full. When
winding, hold the weft tightly so that it almost burns your fingers.
This is necessary especially when winding linen. When using a wool
weft do not wind more than enough bobbins to use up at once
because wool soon loses its elasticity under tension. A wool warp
should be woven off as soon as possible for this same reason.

Our great-grandmothers called bobbins *quills,* for in those days
they were really made of goose quills. Today we usually buy
bobbins and they are made of cardboard or plastic. You can, however, make satisfactory bobbins yourself. Take a rectangular piece
of fairly stiff and smooth wrapping paper, having the diagonal
of the rectangle shorter than the metal shaft in your shuttle. Starting at one corner of this paper, wind it around the shaft of the
bobbin winder. As you do this, insert the end of your weft and
continue to wind. Some weavers buy aluminum or brass tubing for
their bobbins while plastic or wooden spools with flanges are now
on sale in supply houses.

Shuttles

There are shuttles large enough to hold rag strips for rug making,
but most users of four-harness looms prefer the smaller boat

shuttles for both tabby and pattern wefts. Boat shuttles with rollers are more suitable for looms having a shuttle race than with those that do not have this added feature on the beater. (See Glossary). Whether the bottom of the shuttle is open or closed is a matter of preference. Some table looms have narrow sheds, and for them it pays to buy the special small boat shuttles which some supply houses sell.

Heddles

Almost all looms made nowadays have either flat steel or round wire heddles and they should be rustproof. "Old-timey" looms all had string heddles and for some warp yarns string heddles with their large eyes are very useful. They are also less expensive, for you can make them yourself. Make a pattern, called a jig, like Illustration 32. Ten-inch heddles are standard, and the eyes are usually 1 inch long.

If, when you threaded the heddles on to the steel bars of your harnesses, two of them were crossed, do not use either of them when threading your patterns. The skipped heddles will not affect your weaving in any way, unless you are using a great many warp ends to the inch.

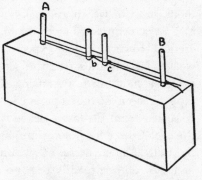

CONCERNING THE LOOM ITSELF

The modern loom for handweavers is different from those used in ancient times, although the principle is the same. Paintings found on ancient pottery

Illustration 32. A pattern or jig for tying many string heddles one on top of the other. The knots are square knots, and the distance between knots at b and c is one inch, forming the eye of the heddle. The distance between A and B varies with the specifications of the loom but is usually somewhere between 10 and 12 inches.

from Greece shows us that their looms were vertical as are the Navajo Indian looms and certain art looms used today. We know that the looms in use in Egypt about four thousand years ago were horizontal and that they had wedge-shaped pegs at the top of them which were driven into the ground, because in the Cairo Museum there is a miniature model of a weaving workshop which was found within the tomb of a Steward of the Royal Palace. It gives us a picture of the daily life of weavers in the valley of the Nile long ago. The servants are shown preparing the flax, spinning it, making a warp on pegs on the wall, just as we do today, and weaving on one of their horizontal looms.

When weavers ask what size of loom to buy, the only possible answer to give is in the form of a question: Where do you live and what do you intend to weave? Small apartments probably mean that a table loom or a small folding loom would be most suitable. But if space is no object, then for general use a 36-inch loom is good to have. On the other hand, if you intend to weave drapery and coverlets, then buy a wider one, 45-inch width at least.

For most weaving, the question of whether to buy a rising shed loom (most of which are jack-type) or a sinking shed loom, known also as a counterbalanced loom, is largely one of personal preference. However, if you expect to weave linen and use the Bronson weave, for instance (see the second part of this book), you may prefer a loom with the rising shed because the harnesses of this type of loom do not operate in pairs as do those of the counterbalanced loom. Bronson weave is a type of weaving which requires the use of three harnesses simultaneously and also of a single harness by itself. The harnesses of a counterbalanced loom operate in pairs and they do not readily respond to irregular tie-ups. However, this objection to the counterbalanced loom has been overcome by one manufacturing concern which now makes a shed regulator which is easily attached to their looms. Whether it can be used with other makes, I do not know.

The question of whether to buy a loom with a sectional beam or not has already been discussed in a previous chapter. Just introduce this subject into a group of weavers and the discussion pro and con will last far, far into the night! Sectional beams certainly do away with a good deal of the work of preparing a warp and make it easy for one person to do it alone. However, in Chapter 5 instructions are given for beaming a warp on a plain beam by anyone who is working without assistance. The best solution to this problem would appear to be the purchase of a sectional beam in addition to the plain beam and to use it when and as you see fit.

The beater of a loom may be suspended from above or fastened below near the floor. Some manufacturers offer both models. Looms used in Europe, especially those in Scandinavia, have the former type as a rule, but in this country we seem to prefer the latter. No matter where the beater is hung, however, form the habit of moving the warp forward frequently and do not weave too close to the reed since it is better to weave within a three or four inch space. This assures that the angle at which the beater strikes the last row of your weaving will remain more constant.

Counterbalanced looms may have their harnesses suspended in various ways. One is by means of what are known as *horses* which are more commonly found on old-fashioned looms and handmade ones. Horses are coat-hanger shaped pieces of wood suspended by cords coming from pulleys in some such fashion as shown in Illustration 33. They take the place of the rollers already described. Edward

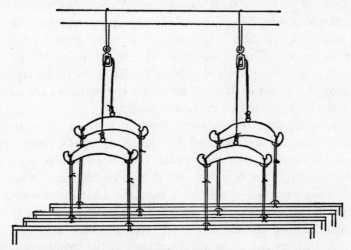

Illustration 33. Attachment of harnesses by means of horses. Snitch knots are used to tie the horses to the harnesses.

F. Worst in his *Foot-Power Loom Weaving,* shows illustrations of this type of harness suspension. If the harnesses work together, they are all right, but all too frequently, at least in my experience, they do not, causing the harnesses to tilt until they look like signals at a railway crossing!

When harnesses are suspended by means of pulleys in place of rollers, the cords often slip down between the pulley housing and the wheel and become so badly jammed that they have to be cut.

The most satisfactory method of harness suspension, therefore, is the one already described in Chapter 1. When rollers are used the movement goes through their full length so that they and the harnesses always remain horizontal.

The height of the breast beam is also something to be considered when buying or building a loom for it should be just high enough to allow your elbows to rest on it as you sit at the loom. Of course, this may be a question of the height of your loom bench. Because there is nothing more fatiguing than to work at a loom which is not the proper height for you, it pays to buy the loom bench along with the loom.

Swedish weavers are emphatic in saying that a loom cannot be less than 72 inches from front to rear. While this distance is an exaggerated one in the opinion of most weavers over here, it is true that too short a distance will not produce good sheds. I have seen some looms where the space from the breast beam to the harnesses was very short while that from the harnesses to the slabstock was long. Keep this in mind: The nearer the harnesses are to half-way from back to front of the loom, the better.

Whether the treadles are better fastened in front or in the rear is also a debated question. If the free ends are in front, better leverage is obtained, but the treadles then often wobble from side to side, making it difficult to find them with the feet. When the treadles are attached at the heel bar this difficulty is overcome, though the weaver does have to reach farther towards the rear of the treadles with the feet for good leverage. Some manufacturers overcome this by extending the fixed ends of the treadles out from the heel bar. This arrangement of "organ type" treadle is very satisfactory and can be seen on the loom shown in the frontispiece.

Most four-harness looms have six treadles so that by tying each one to a combination of two harnesses the usual weaving directions can be followed. This has already been explained in Chapter 7. When a loom has but four treadles, they are tied singly to a harness through the lamm directly above the treadle. Two treadles are then used together to make the necessary harness combinations. It makes no difference whether your loom has four treadles or six, you can weave the same patterns.

Beginners, indeed, make trouble for themselves worrying about tie-ups. When you copy a pattern draft, look for and copy down the treadle tie-up that was used. If it is not the same as your own, transpose it. Remember, it is the *harnesses* that are important, not the number of the treadle. If the directions call for harnesses 1 and 4, then use treadle 6 of the Worst tie-up, etc. If directions are given that call for treadle 2 and you see that their tie-up has this treadle attached to harnesses 3 and 4, then all you do is use the treadle of your tie-up that pulls down harnesses 3 and 4, which in the Worst tie-up is treadle 5. This is assuming that the directions given are for a counterbalanced loom.

When the directions tell you that they are for the jack type or rising shed loom and you have a counterbalanced loom, transpose as follows:

For harnesses 1 & 2 use harnesses 3 & 4 or treadle 5 (Worst)
" " 2 & 3 " " 1 & 4 " " 6 "
" " 3 & 4 " " 1 & 2 " " 1 "
" " 1 & 4 " " 2 & 3 " " 2 "

Or, if you wish, you can use their directions weaving the material wrong side up. The tabby shots do not need to be changed.

For a table loom, any directions given for the rising shed loom will weave the material right side up. The levers are numbered from front to back and when they are pulled down, the harnesses rise, just as they do on a rising shed floor loom. In Chapter 9, directions were given for transposing sinking shed or counterbalanced loom treadling directions into those for a table loom.

We usually say that the lumber in a loom should be of hardwood. Yet many an old loom is still in use today which is made of softwood. However, should you be making your own loom, choose well-seasoned lumber which is free of knots and clear-grained.

Mortises and tenons in the construction of a loom were mentioned in Chapter 1. Today the tendency is to use bolts, for they are cheaper and serve as well, if not better. There is the added advantage that they have no wooden tenons to bump your shins against.

Many looms come equipped with aprons, but some do not. You can easily make your own, following Illustrations 15 and 16 on pages 54 and 55, or you can use the method of attaching long doubled cords shown in Illustration 17. Aprons make a neater job of it and are to be preferred to cords which will make unsightly ridges in your first piece of weaving on a warp.

Weavers very often forget to take into consideration the noise that a loom may make. The *thump, thump, thump* of a loom beater is to the weaver a pleasing sound, but it may be most annoying to others in the household. Sponge rubber cemented at the points on the loom uprights where the beater strikes will often bring peace to the family.

Walking looms are also a nuisance for some are inclined to travel all over the room. You can buy loom treads to put under the corner posts of your loom but I have found that suede leather tied or tacked around the posts like little boots work just as well.

Together we have come a considerable distance along the road to good weaving. I hope that you have found it a pleasant journey and that you will wish to continue as my companion for the rest of the way.

Part Two is to "grow on." Happy weaving!

PART TWO

A DISCUSSION OF VARIOUS WEAVES
FOR FOUR-HARNESS LOOMS

"The lyf so short, the craft so long to learn."
Chaucer

Chapter 11

THE TWILL WEAVE

The simplest threading possible on a four-harness loom is twill. This is also the threading used when you wish to weave entirely in plain weave. Twill on four harnesses is usually threaded 4.3.2.1 all across the width of the warp or 1.2.3.4 all the way across.

Twills are characterized by diagonals called *wales* going across the fabric. The best known four-harness twill is the 2–2 twill, the figures referring to the number of skipped threads on the two sides of the material. It is produced by tromping * the pattern treadles in order over and over again (i.e., treadles 1.2.5.6 Diagram 4, page 78, the Worst tie-up) and is usually woven with one shuttle only and no tabby. If you desire to change the direction of the wales, change the order of tromping to 6.5.2.1.

Another twill is the 3–1 twill with the opposite side of the fabric a 1–3 twill. The tie-up on page 118 is for the 3–1 twill, and is threaded, woven, and treadled the same as the 2–2 twill. The tabby treadles (3 and 4) are not as a rule used.

---

* This dialectal variant of the verb *to treadle* is used from now on to eliminate the confusion which often arises because of the similarity in print of the words *treadling* and *threading*. It is a visual aid only and not intended necessarily that you use it in your speech.

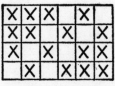

6 5 4 3 2 1

Diagram 6.

This tie-up is for a counterbalanced loom with a sinking shed. For a loom with rising shed (table, jack type, etc.) and also to weave the 1–3 twill uppermost on the counterbalanced loom, use the blank spaces of this tie-up. If you use the tie-up intended for the counterbalanced loom on the rising shed loom, the 1–3 twill will be uppermost.

A herringbone twill is one in which the direction of the wales changes where the threading of the draft is reversed, as follows:

BEGIN

REPEAT FROM BEGINNING AS DESIRED

Diagram 7.

Herringbones may be tromped the same as the 2–2, 3–1 or 1–3 twills. Broken twills and broken herringbones are those in which the diagonals do not appear because the order of tromping is broken up by transposing the order of use of two of the treadles, as for instance, when tromping treadles 1.2.6.5 of the Worst tie-up, Chapter 7.

Mixed twills and herringbones are those which are tromped using the tabby treadles before and after each of the twill trompings.

When a herringbone is woven, there is seen at each point of the design a three-thread weft skip. These skips are often undesirable, especially in upholstery material, because they may catch on clothing so a threading known as a dornick twill is often used which eliminates them. In dornick twills the diagonals still go in opposite directions, but they do not meet to form a point as they do in herringbones. Opposite is a draft for a dornick twill. Notice that there is a threading of a harness omitted between warp ends number 2 and 3 and between warp ends number 8 and 9. In this way, the skips are eliminated.

Dornick twills are usually woven by tromping treadles 1. 2. 5 and 6 (Worst tie-up) over and over again. Because of the peculiarity of the threading mentioned before, there can be no true tabby (treadles 3 and 4) because, wherever there is a threading on harness 3 followed by a threading on harness 1 and one on harness 2 followed by a threading on harness 4, there will occur a flat in the tabby sheds. This, however, cannot be avoided.

		4			4				4
	3					3		3	
2			2				2		
1					1			1	

REPEAT AS DESIRED

Diagram 8.

All tartans are woven in 2–2 twill. The beautiful effects are produced by a regular sequence of color stripes both in the warp and in the weft.

When weaving twills do not be disturbed by the fact that the outside warp end is not being caught by the weft, for this is characteristic of the weave. If the fabric is woven so that the wales continue to slant in one direction for the entire length of the piece, then there will be an outside warp end which hangs free, but if the wales are reversed, by reversing the order of tromping the treadles, at that point the edge will be caught. This unwoven outside warp end can be overcome by using two shuttles each carrying the same weft. With the first shuttle weave one row from right to left, change the shed and weave the next row from right to left with the second shuttle. Continue to alternate shuttles.

To weave a twill with one shuttle so that a warp end hangs free is, however, a good check on your tromping, for, if a treadle is skipped, you will know it instantly by the fact that the outside selvage thread is caught by the weft.

Chapter references: For a much more detailed discussion of twills, see Marguerite P. Davison's *A Handweaver's Pattern Book*, revised edition, also Oscar A. Bériau's *Home Weaving* (English), *Le Métier à Quatre Lames* in French, and *Twills, Tweeds and Other All Wool Fabrics* (Shuttle Craft Guild).

Chapter 12

THE OVERSHOT WEAVE

The overshot weave has been in use for centuries and is as popular today as ever. Most of the old coverlets woven with four harnesses were done on drafts of overshot. Their very names are intriguing: Whig Rose and Lover's Knot, Chariot Wheels or Church Windows, Windflower, Orange Peel, Lee's Surrender, Star of the Sea and Federal Knot. We wonder what weavers named them long ago! From diaries and old letters we know that, just as recipes are exchanged today, the old coverlet drafts went from hand to hand. Smaller patterns are just as numerous with Honeysuckle, Rose Path, and Monk's Belt leading the long list.

The overshot weave is so called because of the "overshots" called *floats* made by the colored pattern weft where it skips over certain portions of the warp. These floats contribute beauty and color to the weave but are its greatest weakness. Many times an old piece of weaving will remain intact except for the places where the floats of color have been worn away. These skips of weft over warp catch on clothing, too, so it is not practical to have long floats occur in a draft. Not many overshot drafts are written for more than four harnesses as it is typically a four-harness weave.

Today we are quite likely to use any weft we choose but most of the old coverlets were woven with wool. The warp was of linen, for not until about 1830 was machinery introduced for spinning cotton warp.

HOW TO TROMP AN OVERSHOT

On a four-harness loom the combinations used for tromping an overshot pattern are made up of two harnesses used together, as follows: (but not necessarily in this order) 1 & 2; 2 & 3; 3 & 4; and 1 & 4, corresponding to treadles 1, 2, 5, and 6 of the Worst tie-up, page 78. Tabby or plain weave is woven by tromping harnesses 1 & 3 together for one tabby shot and 2 & 4 together for the other (treadles 3 and 4 alternately). If you are not already familiar with the method of weaving with two shuttles, see page 95.

The draft given below is for the Honeysuckle pattern. It can be tromped in so many ways that one might say the possibilities are endless. There are 26 warp ends in each repeat of the draft as follows:

HONEYSUCKLE

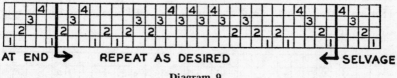

AT END ➡ REPEAT AS DESIRED ⬅ SELVAGE

Diagram 9.

Examining this draft, note that nowhere do you see a 1 next to a 3 or a 2 next to a 4. These are tabby combinations and are seldom written in a draft for the overshot weave. But if you pick out the alternate warp ends in the draft—there they are! Therefore, by tromping the odd-numbered warp ends together by the use of treadle 3 you have one tabby shed while the even-numbered ends (treadle 4) give you the other. The other combinations are reserved for the pattern shots.

If you are using Mr. Worst's book, *Foot-Power Loom Weaving*, however, you will find in it some drafts for the overshot weave in which the tabby treadles are to be tied to harnesses 1 & 2 and 3 & 4, so that the usual tabby combinations of 1 & 3, and 2 & 4 do occur in these drafts as pattern shots. This will not disturb the experienced weaver, but the beginner will need to pay strict attention to the instructions given with these drafts in order to treadle them correctly.

If you have a draft for the overshot weave but have no tromping directions for it, it does not really matter except in the case of the coverlets, and a few other drafts which are tromped in a traditional way. But, for most drafts, it is fun to make up your own tromping, writing down the treadle numbers you use as you go along so that the pleasing ones may be repeated. Remember, overshot drafts are usually woven with two shuttles, one with tabby weft, the other carrying a coarser pattern weft, in color, as a general rule.

Many overshot drafts are prettiest when woven "as drawn in," or as expressed in the speech of the Southern Appalachian Highlands, when they are "tromped as writ." This simply means that the harness combinations found in the written draft are taken for the tromping of it. Let us encircle the harness combinations in the Honeysuckle draft because from this you can get the tromping for Honeysuckle "woven as drawn in." You will not need to encircle the selvage.

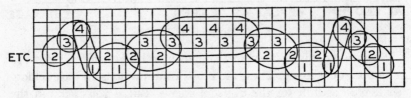

Diagram 10.

Beginning at the right, the first combination found is the 1 & 2. Then comes 2 & 3 (the 2 is common to both) followed by 3 & 4, and the next one is 1 & 4. The next is a 1 & 2, and in it there are four warp ends so they are encircled as are the four warp ends on the 2 & 3 coming next. The largest combination in this pattern draft is the 3 & 4 which comes next, for in it there are 7 warp ends. (That is, at that point, when the draft was threaded through the heddles, seven warp ends were divided between these two harnesses.)

This is the center of the pattern and you can readily see that from here on the draft reverses.

Instead of saying "combinations" in the previous paragraphs, we could have said "blocks" and meant the same thing. The blocks in this weave form the floats, for when they are woven the color weft skips over the warp. The size of the float, therefore, depends upon how many warp ends there were threaded to the block and also how coarse or fine a reed you are using. For example if the Honeysuckle draft after being threaded were sleyed one to a dent in a reed with only ten dents per inch, it can readily be seen that this large 3–4 block would be 7/10 of an inch long—too long to be practical.

But now let us return to the question of finding out how to weave this draft "tromped as writ."

The first block encircled on the right has only two figures (corresponding to warp ends) in it. The next three blocks also have two in each. But the fifth block written on 1 and 2 has four warp ends in it: 1,2,1,2. When you tromp as writ, the general rule to follow is: Repeat the tromping for one less time than the number of warp ends in the block in question.

Therefore, here is the tromping: (Use a tabby before *and* after each pattern shot.)

Harnesses 1 & 2 (tr. 1)	once
" 2 & 3 (tr. 2)	once
" 3 & 4 (tr. 5)	once
" 1 & 4 (tr. 6)	once
" 1 & 2	3 times
" 2 & 3	3 times *
" 3 & 4	6 times

and reverse beginning at *

There is no law that says you must tromp each combination the number of times indicated, so if you do not like it, change it to suit yourself.

We have already noted on page 122 that certain figures in the draft were common to two successive tromping (that is, harness) combinations. You will notice that in the tromping directions given before for Honeysuckle there is also one figure common to two successive pattern trompings, for instance, harnesses 1 & 2; followed by 2 & 3, etc. This holds true for any overshot pattern unless it is woven *on opposites*. See below.

The tromping which we worked out is only one of many which are possible for Honeysuckle. To find others, play around with the treadles to discover what combinations are pleasing to you. One way to find variations is by the use of a lady's pocket mirror. Place the mirror on edge next to the last row of weaving and you will see in it how the design would appear if the tromping were to be reversed at that point. When you reverse a tromping direction, always have an even number of repeats of the pattern shot you used for the reversal point so that the same tabby shed is coupled with the same pattern shot for the entire tromping. Remember, too, that there are *fourteen* tromping combinations possible with a four-harness loom for, in addition to those of the regular tie-up, it is possible to change the tie-up so that each harness is used alone or so that three harnesses are used together. With these irregular tie-ups, however, the counterbalanced loom is at a disadvantage. Refer to page 143.

Many of the old colonial designs, especially those for coverlets, were woven so that each block which occurred on the diagonal of the design became a square, hence the term *square the diagonal*. If this is done, the remainder of the design will take care of itself. This is especially true of the circular patterns, whose blocks vary in size, but all those occurring on the diagonal are woven until they are square. To find the blocks on the diagonal, encircle the combinations as you did for the Honeysuckle draft. Write down the harness combinations just the same as before. When determining the number of times to repeat each combination, however, watch the material you are weaving to see that the blocks on the diagonal of the design are made square. The number of repeats of each harness combination to make naturally depends upon the type of weft you are using, how closely the warp is sleyed, and how hard you are beating.

Any overshot draft may also be woven "on opposites," if desired.

Some, indeed, are seldom if ever woven in any other way. Monk's Belt is a typical example.

MONK'S BELT

REPEAT AS DESIRED

Diagram 11.

When threading this draft, after the last pattern repeat has been threaded, end with the first ten warp ends.

To weave this draft usually the only harness combinations employed are those of the 1 & 2 and 3 & 4 harnesses (treadles 1 and 5). These are "opposite" combinations for 1 & 2 are the two front harnesses while 3 & 4 are the two towards the rear of the loom. The other two opposite combinations (the two middle harnesses, 2 & 3, and the two outer ones, 1 & 4 i.e., treadles 2 and 6, page 78), are not used at all in Monk's Belt as a general rule.

The following are two variations for Monk's Belt borders. Use a tabby before and after the pattern shots.

1. Tr. 1..8 times	2. Tr. 1..2 times ⎫ Repeat these
" 5..4 times	" 5..2 times ⎭ 3 times
" 1..8 times	" 1..8 times
	" 5..4 times
	" 1..8 times
	" 5..2 times ⎫ Repeat these
	" 1..2 times ⎭ 3 times

Monk's Belt may be woven in two colors. Use one for shots on treadle 1 and the other for those on treadle 5—three shuttles in all.

The effect given by weaving on opposites is severe and clean-cut. In the background of the woven material, there is found none of the small flecks of color which occur when a draft is tromped in the usual manner.

Notice that opposite harness combinations do not have a number in common. The tromping of harnesses 1 & 2 together is followed by 3 & 4 together but never by 2 & 3 or 1 & 4. If, for instance, the combination 1 & 4 (Tr. 6) is used, it would be followed by its opposite, 2 & 3 (treadle 2) and not by any of the others. This, then, is what is meant by "weaving on opposites." Try it on any overshot pattern.

Sometimes technical discussions for a draft woven on opposites make mention of "accidentals." This is a term used to refer to the harness combinations which, while written in the draft, are not as a rule tromped. For instance, in the Monk's Belt draft, the combinations of 2 & 3 and 1 & 4 can be seen if you encircle the draft as was done with Honeysuckle on page 122. These warp ends must be threaded through the heddles but when it comes to tromping the pattern, they are not ordinarily used. If they were omitted from the threading, however, you would have a 1 & 3 and a 2 & 4 combination appearing in the draft. Then, when tabby was tromped, two warp ends in adjacent heddles would find themselves either on the top or the bottom of the shed together. This makes an error in weaving called a "flat." (See page 83.) So, while accidentals must be threaded, they are not tromped if the pattern is woven on opposites.

Bound weaving is also an interesting method to try. For this you will need four shuttles, each one carrying a different harmonizing color, or you may like to use four shades of one color. The wefts should all be the same grist. Use no tabby. Tromp the treadles 1.2.5 and 6 over and over again, a different shuttle being thrown with each treadle. Start all four shuttles from the right and as each one is used lay it in front of you, one under the other, so that they are all kept in order ready for use again. The wefts are carried up the selvages. Keep a strong tension on the warp when weaving in this manner.

If at any time you wish to move the color of a stripe to another position, change the order of the shuttles but keep the tromping the same.

The fabric produced will be quite heavy and weft-faced, the warp except at hem or fringe, will be entirely covered on both sides of the material. For this reason, the warp must be sleyed fairly far apart and the wefts must be such that they will slip down along the warp ends and cover them. Carpet warp, one to a dent in a 15-dent reed, used with #3 pearl cotton for the wefts, is quite satisfactory. I have also seen this method used for material for purses on the Rose Path draft using 20/2 cotton warp yarn. The warp was threaded two ends through each heddle and two in a dent of a 12-dent reed. The weft used was a fine worsted yarn, and the warp did not show. Bound weaving requires time and patience, because there are many, many rows of weaving in each inch of material. But it is rewarding.

This type of material shrinks when off the loom both in length and width and this fact must be taken into consideration when planning the warp. Interesting pattern effects can be worked out by the way in which the colors are rotated.

The next method of weaving an overshot I shall designate as "Honeycomb weaving," in spite of the fact that I know that some weavers contend it is not true honeycomb. It is a type of weaving in which one may say that there is a third dimension, for it is characterized by horizontal rows of sunken spots separated by two wavy, heavy, tabby shots. On the right side of the web there are a few short skips in the warp and on the wrong side there appear long, unsightly weft skips producing a decidedly one-sided material. Monk's Belt and Honeysuckle can both be woven this way as can, in fact, any overshot pattern where the blocks are fairly large and drafted neither too close nor too far apart.

WEAVING DIRECTIONS FOR A HONEYCOMB

Counterbalanced loom. First choose your wefts. Contrary to the usual practice, the tabby thread must be heavier than the pattern weft. Carpet warp for the tabby in white or natural with a colored weft in a grist about that of 20/2 cotton is suggested for use on a fine (20/2) cotton warp. After the hem is woven, weave as follows: (The Worst tie-up will have to be changed to the direct tie-up given in Chapter 7. Tabby is woven by using two treadles together: 1 & 3; 2 & 4.) Directions are for the counterbalanced loom. Keep

the tension of the warp as soft as compatible with a good shed and
beat the tabby shots hard.

Block A. Harness 1...once ⎫ Alternate these two rows about ten times
         Harness 2...once ⎭ using the fine weft. No tabby.

Follow with two rows of tabby with the heavy weft.

Block B. Harness 3...once ⎫
         Harness 4...once ⎭ alternate same as above.

Two rows of heavy tabby.

Block C. Harness 1...once ⎫ alternate as above.
         Harness 4...once ⎭

Two rows of heavy tabby.

Block D. Harness 2...once ⎫ as above.
         Harness 3...once ⎭

Two rows of heavy tabby.

If you are weaving this on the Monk's Belt threading, perhaps
you will not care for the effect given by Blocks C and D. The other
two blocks are the ones usually used with this draft.

Honeycomb weaving shrinks greatly both in width and length
when off the loom and after it is laundered. The shrinkage in
length is almost 20%.

For a loom with rising shed, which is better for this irregular
tie-up, substitute as follows:

> For harness 1...use harnesses or levers 2, 3 and 4 together
> For harness 2... "   "   "   " 1, 3 and 4   "
> For harness 3... "   "   "   " 1, 2 and 4   "
> For harness 4... "   "   "   " 1, 2 and 3   "

Any overshot pattern may also be woven in what is known as
"the Italian manner" and this is also an effective way to weave a
Crackle weave pattern (see page 152).

Three shuttles are needed for Italian weaving, each one using a
different color but usually the same grist of weft. One of the
shuttles carries the dominant color; the other two are backgrounds.

The two background colors "may be strongly contrasted in shade but should not be too far apart in value, and should be a good deal lighter than the pattern color." *

My artistic friends tell me that examples of such colors would be: gray and pale yellow; purple and yellow; red-violet and blue-violet with yellow-green for the main color; pale olive green and cold gray and with this a vermilion for the dominant color.

We shall designate these shuttles as P, B1 and B2. The effect gained is somewhat similar to the flame or Bargello type of embroidery.

Draw a circle on a piece of paper and on its circumference mark the four usual pattern harness combinations as follows:

Place this where you can see it as you weave.

Now refer to the tromping directions for Honeysuckle on page 123, and we will weave this pattern in the Italian manner. The first instruction calls for harnesses 1 & 2 (treadle 1)—once. Proceed as follows:

Weave harnesses 1 & 2 (together) once with P. Then look along the

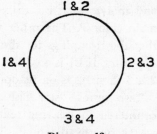

Diagram 12.

circumference of your circle to the next combination there, 2 & 3, and weave it once with B1. Look back again to the original 1 & 2 combination and weave it once with P. Then trace to the left from 1 & 2 at the top of the circle to find 1 & 4 which is your next tromping for which you are to use B2. Then come back to the top of the circle to 1 & 2 and weave it again with P. These five combinations used in this order constitute the first tromping direction of the original Honeysuckle: 1 & 2—once. Start all three shuttles from the right and after use lay them down in front of you in order, ready to be used again.

Here, then, are the tromping equivalents of the four combinations of the harnesses when woven in the Italian manner:

* Mary M. Atwater. *Notes on the Crackle Weave*. Published in Practical Weaving Suggestions, Vol. V#2, Lily Mills Company, Shelby, North Carolina. (Out of print.)

for 1 & 2 read:	for 2 & 3 read:	for 3 & 4 read:	for 1 & 4 read:
1 & 2...P	2 & 3...P	3 & 4...P	1 & 4...P
2 & 3...B1	3 & 4...B1	1 & 4...B1	1 & 2...B1
1 & 2...P	2 & 3...P	3 & 4...P	1 & 4...P
1 & 4...B2	1 & 2...B2	2 & 3...B2	3 & 4...B2
1 & 2...P *	2 & 3...P *	3 & 4...P *	1 & 4...P *

* On the last repeat only.

The figures above refer to *harness combinations*. Substitute the corresponding treadles of your tie-up for them. Of course, all this elongates the design enormously and you may, therefore, decide not to make as many repetitions of the trompings as were given in the original.

To save your sanity and help you greatly, let us look at this and analyze what we really are doing. We have one shuttle with the main color P. The other two are background colors. Now notice that the trompings for the background colors are in every case *on opposites*. If B1 is on 3 & 4 then B2 is tromped on 1 & 2; if B1 is on 2 & 3 then B2 is on its opposite, 1 & 4. Easy now, isn't it?

Two terms, "star fashion" and "rose fashion," are often encountered in weaving text books. To weave "star fashion" is to weave on the diagonal or "tromped as writ," see page 122. To weave "rose fashion" is just the opposite; there is no diagonal and the tromping is inverted to bring this about.

Diagram 13 below shows the regular Worst tie-up and Diagram 14 shows it inverted. The tabby treadles are not changed and the order of tromping and number of shots that were used to tromp your pattern on the diagonal is kept the same.

REGULAR WORST TIE-UP

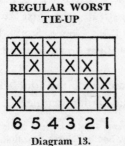

6 5 4 3 2 1

Diagram 13.

INVERTED TIE-UP

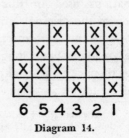

6 5 4 3 2 1

Diagram 14.

A further inversion can also be made by changing the tie-up in Diagram 14. Take the sixth treadle and make it the first; then push the ties of the other pattern treadles along to the left as follows:

In each case the tromping which was used for weaving star fashion or tromped as writ is maintained, but the tie-up is changed or the proper treadle substituted. Do not forget, however, that if you have a loom with a rising shed, the treadles should be tied to the blank spaces in the tie-ups—that is, if you wish to have the material woven right side up.

ANOTHER INVERTED TIE-UP

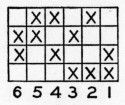

Diagram 15.

Some overshot patterns when woven all or partially in rose fashion have different names as, for example, when Lover's Knot becomes Whig Rose on the same threading. When a draft is to be woven other than as drawn in ("tromped as writ"), you will almost without exception find that the complete tromping directions are given with the draft.

Chapter 13

THE SUMMER AND WINTER WEAVE

Apparently this is a weave of American origin although its discovery near Germantown, Pennsylvania, hints at a Germanic origin. With the coming of machine-made textiles, weaving in the home died out as we know, and this was one of the first weaves to be forgotten. Mrs. Mary M. Atwater was the one to rediscover how it was woven.

It is well named. One side of the material shows up the dark colors, the other shows more of the light—one side for winter, the other for summer! Blue on white was a favorite color combination in old pieces.

Summer and winter is a weave in which there occur no skips of weft over warp of more than three warp ends. This "over-three-under-one" makes for extreme durability. The ease with which the drafts are threaded and woven is also greatly in its favor. It is excellent for upholstery material and other items where wearing quality is of first consideration.

Below is an incomplete draft of a summer and winter:

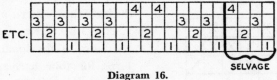

Diagram 16.

You can readily see from this that in the summer and winter weave there is no objection to the 1 & 3; 2 & 4 threading combinations as there was in the overshot weave. Note also that one-half of the warp ends are threaded on harnesses 1 and 2, while all the others are distributed upon the remaining harnesses.

Summer and winter is but one of the weaves that are threaded in what are known as "units." In a four-harness summer and winter draft there are two units threaded as follows: (the warp ends within each unit remain always in the order given). Read as usual in draft writing from right to left.

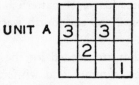

Diagram 17.

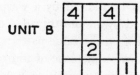

Diagram 18.

The warp ends threaded on harnesses 1 and 2 are known as "tie-down threads." The others are the pattern warp ends. Unit A may also be spoken of as "Unit on 3" because 3 is the harness that carries its pattern warp ends, while Unit B is sometimes called "Unit on 4."

If harnesses 1 & 2 are tromped together for one shot of weft and harnesses 3 & 4 for the return shot, the result will be plain weave (tabby) in a four-harness summer and winter. Diagram 19 gives the tie-up used for this weave, treadles 1 and 2 being tabbies.

Many beautiful drafts have been written in summer and win-

UNIT UNIT
  B   A

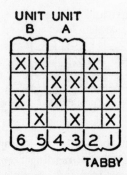

TABBY

Diagram 19. Tie-up for a summer and winter. This is for a counterbalanced loom. For a jack-type loom tie-up to the blank spaces. Table looms use levers as indicated by the blanks.

ter weave for looms with more than four harnesses. In these drafts, the other units are: 1.5.2.5; 1.6.2.6., etc., for as many harnesses as the loom has. Patterns for four harnesses, being limited to two units, are quite geometrical. Note that the number of units possible in a summer and winter draft is always "number of harnesses minus two," because the tie-down threads, which eliminate long floats of weft over warp, use two of the available harnesses.

Drafts for this weave are very seldom written out in full because the regularity of the threading of the units lends itself to a type of shorthand. A unit always consists of four warp ends . . . one on harness 1 followed by a warp end threaded on a pattern harness, followed by an end threaded on harness 2 and the fourth warp end threaded on the same pattern harness.

Two rows in place of four are all that are needed for the shorthand method of writing a four-harness summer and winter. The solid squares each stand for a unit, as, for instance:

Diagram 20.

expanded this would read:

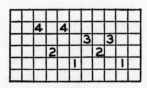

Diagram 21.

To indicate repetitions of these units, simply repeat the solid squares as below:

Diagram 22.

which means that Unit A is to be threaded three times, followed by Unit B twice. The total number of warp ends necessary is twelve for the A units and 8 for the B. The units may be repeated any number of times and, because there are no skips of weft over more than three warp ends, there can be no long floats.

So much for the threading and shorthand drafts for summer and winter. Now for the weaving of them. Below are four different methods.

1. Singles: Tromp as follows, using two shuttles, one carrying a tabby weft the same as or similar to the warp, the other heavier and in a color. Summer and winter weaves beautifully with a homespun type of wool but equally well with cotton, linen and other fibers. Use the tie-up in Diagram 19.

First, weave with treadles 1 and 2 alternately for a hem. *End on treadle 1 from the right.* When weaving with the pattern shuttle, alternate the tabby treadles before and after pattern shots just as in overshot weaving.

> For Unit A: Tr. 3 . . once (start shuttle from the right)
> " 4 . . once
> " 3 . . once
> " 4 . . once
> For Unit B: Tr. 5 . . once (from the right)
> " 6 . . once
> " 5 . . once
> " 6 . . once

Repeat or alternate the weaving of these units in any way desired, or in the order in which they appear in the draft. Four pattern shots and four alternating tabby shots comprise each unit of weaving. Characteristic of this method of weaving a summer and winter are the o's or circular spaces seen in the pattern.

2. Doubles or "in pairs." End with a shot of tabby from right to left on treadle 1 as before. Then:

for Unit A: Tr. 3.. once (from the right)
" 4.. once
" 4.. once
" 3.. once
for Unit B: Tr. 5.. once (from the right)
" 6.. once
" 6.. once
" 5.. once

Tabbies alternate as usual and units are repeated or alternated according to the draft. Weaving in this fashion gives a "bricky" background which many weavers prefer to the other.

3. Corded or ribbed effect. In this method we use but one of the two possible treadles for each unit but not the other. (Either one may be used.) End the weaving of a hem on tabby treadle 1 from the right, and keep on alternating tabbies as usual.

Unit A: Tr. 3 ... four times   Unit B: Tr. 5 ... four times
or Tr. 4   *or* Tr. 6

This method is more effective in drafts written for multiple harness looms.

4. Without a tabby. This produces an effect the same as Bound Weaving (page 126). Careful selection of the warp and its sett in the reed and also of the type of weft produces a weft-faced material, that is, one in which no warp shows except at hems and fringes. It is very effective for baby blankets when done in a fine wool warp and weft. Sley the warp in the reed about 15–18 ends to the inch. Use two colors of weft and no tabby.

Tr. 3 ... blue; once
" 5 ... pink; once
" 4 ... blue; once
" 6 ... pink; once

Repeat these four rows until the pink and blue checks are square. To change the position of the color checks, switch over to the pink on treadle 3 (two rows of pink occurring together). The warp is threaded with a selvage (see draft page 133) then Unit A and Unit B are threaded alternately all across the warp for small squares or two or more repeats of each unit for larger squares. By maintaining the color order with no change, one may weave stripes instead of squares.

Please note that the methods of weaving given here for the summer and winter weave are to be woven by themselves. They do not combine well, as a rule, in a single piece of weaving.

Chapter 14

THE M'S AND O'S WEAVE

M's and O's is a weave used in this country chiefly for linens although in Europe it is often used for heavier materials, woolens and even rugs. One can easily see the "O's" in the weaving; the "M's" are harder to find. It is a weave which produces material alike on both sides. Warp and weft are traditionally of the same fiber but nowadays we like to experiment with combinations. It is usually woven *square count,* that is, with the same number of rows of weft per inch as there are warp ends in each inch, but here again weavers do as they please.

Sleyed in the reed at 36 warp ends per inch for either 40/2 linen warp or 20/2 cotton warp; or at 40 to 45 ends per inch for 50/2 linen or 24/2 cotton, M's and O's is more beautiful than when in a coarser setting.

M's and O's is a weave for four harnesses and, like summer and winter, is threaded in units which may be repeated or alternated in the draft as desired. It is possible also to make pleasing modifications of the weave by varying the number of warp ends in each of the two units. Usually the units of M's and O's are threaded with eight warp ends each as follows:

138

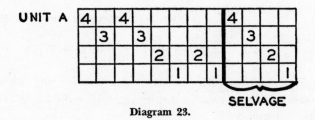

Diagram 23.

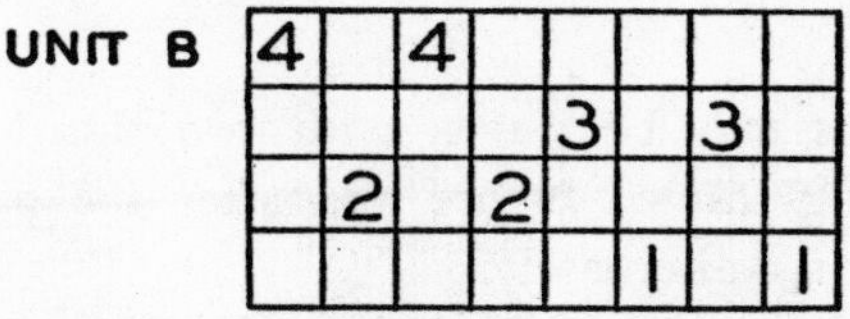

Diagram 24.

These eight-thread units may be combined in one and the same draft with four-thread units written 1234 for Unit A and 1324 for Unit B. Sometimes twelve-thread units are seen (121212343434 and 131313242424) but these are less common and, unless sleyed closely in the reed, produce long skips of weft over warp which might be undesirable.

As in the summer and winter weave, the order of the threading of the warp ends within each unit is never changed.

The following is the tie-up of the treadles for this weave:

There is no true tabby possible in this weave. The nearest approach comes from tromping tr. 5 alternately with tr. 6. This gives a dainty effect for hems.

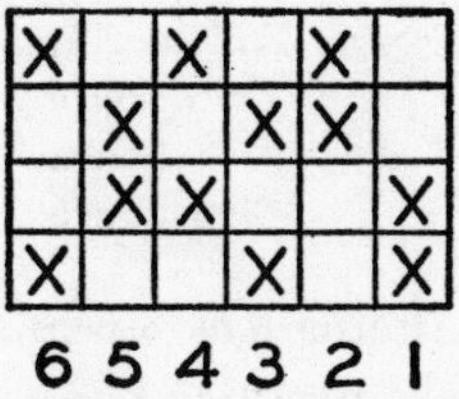

HOW TO TROMP
AN M'S AND O'S

This is a one-shuttle weave. Usually eight picks (rows) are required to weave each unit, unless the weft is very fine or very coarse.

6 5 4 3 2 1

Diagram 25. Tie-up for M's and O's for the counterbalanced loom. The jack type can use the same tie-up.

For Unit A: Tr. 1...once⎱ Alternate four times (8 shots); no tabby.
           Tr. 2...once⎰

For Unit B: Tr. 3...once⎱ Alternate four times (8 shots); no tabby.
           Tr. 4...once⎰

The units may be woven in any order or with any amount of repetition desired, but usually it is best to follow the order in which they appear in the draft.

Variations

1. M's and O's may be woven with two shuttles, the "tabby" shuttle being thrown before and after the pattern shots on treadles 5 and 6 alternately.

2. Try weaving an M's and O's in two colors. For Unit A this would be as follows:

> Tr. 1 then 2...twice with first color
> Tr. 1 then 2...once with second color
> Tr. 1 then 2...twice with first color

3. Woven in the Bronson manner, an M's and O's so closely resembles a Bronson (see page 142) that it is often necessary to turn the material over to see which it is. Use one shuttle, no "tabby," except where indicated.

Unit A:	Tr. 1..once⎱ Repeat	Unit B:	Tr. 3..once⎱ Repeat
	Tr. 2..once⎰		Tr. 4..once⎰
	Followed by		Followed by
	Tr. 5..once		Tr. 5..once
	" 6..once		" 6..once
	" 5..once		" 5..once

Alternate or repeat units as desired. Use a linen weft.

4. Twill treadling of an M's and O's: This is largely for a texture effect. Tromp the treadles in order over and over again using but one shuttle. Treadles 5 and 6 are optional.

The threading for an M's and O's combines very well with twill and herringbone in a draft. For a pretty example see the "E. F.

Towel," in Mary M. Atwater's book, *The Shuttle-Craft Book of American Hand-Weaving.*

Short Draft for M's and O's: Very often, as was seen in the discussion of the summer and winter weave, a weaver wishes to save time and space in draft-writing. We know that the first unit of this weave contains 8 warp ends always threaded the same: 1,2,1,2,3,4,3,4 (reading from left to right); while the second unit reads: 1,3,1,3,2,4,- 2,4.

It therefore becomes very easy to make a short draft for this weave:

The solid squares stand for the units and represent 8 warp ends each, threaded as given on page 139. This diagram is not a complete pattern but is merely to show you how easy it is to make your own drafts by using this shorthand method.

Diagram 26.

Chapter references: For an excellent discussion of short drafts see "The Profile System of Writing Drafts" by Helen L. Allen and Osma Gallinger which is one of the *Practical Weaving Suggestions* published by the Lily Mills Company, Shelby, North Carolina.

Chapter 15

THE BRONSON OR
SPOT WEAVE

The Bronson weave was brought to the attention of weavers in a now very rare little volume entitled "The Domestic Manufacturer's Assistant," written in 1817 by two brothers, J. & R. Bronson. To the bibliophile the original edition of this book would be a choice addition to the library shelves for there are very few known copies in existence. It was reprinted in 1949 and published by the Charles T. Branford Company of Boston, Mass. The reprint shows it to be a very quaint book indeed with its archaic idiom and spelling.

Bronson is a one-shuttle weave well adapted for use with linen. Characteristic are the warp skips on one side of the fabric and the weft skips on the other. Either side may be the "right side" according to your preference. Typically the warp and weft should be of the same grist, color and fiber and the beating adjusted for square count. For towels, luncheon sets, etc., a 40/2 linen warp at 30 to 36 warp ends per inch is very pretty. For weft a 20/1 linen or a 16/1 (coarser) is suggested.

Because of the irregular tie-up, this is a weave better woven on looms having independent harness action such as the jack type and table looms unless the counterbalanced loom has a shed regulator.

There are two forms of Bronson: the original or Point Bronson, which is sometimes referred to as Barleycorn, and the Lace Bronson.

POINT BRONSON

In a Point Bronson draft written for four harnesses, three threading units are available, threaded as follows:

First unit	1.2.1.2	(read from left to right)
Second unit	1.3.1.3	" " " " "
Third unit	1.4.1.4	" " " " "

Thus each unit consists of four warp ends, except when the warp is sleyed through the reed very closely, then as many as ten warp ends may be in one unit. Note that the odd-numbered warp ends are all on harness 1 while the even-numbered ones are distributed among the other harnesses. This gives you harness 1 for the first tabby (every other warp end) while harnesses 2, 3 and 4 tromped together give you the other. This is also true for the Lace Bronson. In the Bronson weave the tabbies are usually designated as Tabby A and Tabby B.

The following is the tie-up for a four-harness Point Bronson on a counterbalanced loom. For a jack type or other loom with a rising shed, tie the treadles, or use the levers of a table loom, as indicated by the o's.

This is an example of what is called an irregular tie-up because some of the harnesses are not tied to the treadles two by two. These tie-ups are not ideal for a counterbalanced loom, therefore a shed regulator is advisable. Such a regulator is shown in a sketch given in the "Master Weaver," No. 10, a mimeographed periodical from Z-Handicrafts, Fulford, Quebec, Canada. This shed regulator is now available for the LeClerc Looms manufactured in Canada.

TIE-UP FOR BRONSON

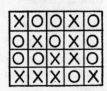

Diagram 27.

A peculiarity of the tromping of a Point Bronson is, that except for hems in plain weave, the *A* tabby treadle is very seldom used. Trompings for the three units are as follows:

Unit 1: Tr. 1 once followed by Tabby B with same shuttle
        Tr. 1   "   "   "   "   "   "   "   "
Unit 2: Tr. 2 once followed by Tabby B with same shuttle
        Tr. 2   "   "   "   "   "   "   "   "
Unit 3: Tr. 3 once followed by Tabby B with same shuttle
        Tr. 3   "   "   "   "   "   "   "   "

These units are usually woven in the same order in which they occur in the draft, but this is not a hidebound rule.

If it is desired to have areas of plain weave surround the "spots," these areas are threaded 1.2.1.2.1.2 etc. for the width of the area desired. Then, in this case only units 2 and 3 are available for the pattern shots. Such a draft would appear like this:

Diagram 28.

For a complete draft, thread alternately a plain area and the units as shown above for the width desired.

Tromping directions for this Point Bronson are as follows:

Start shuttle at the right.
Hem: A.B.A.B.A.B., etc., ending on B.
Unit 2: (the first unit is not used with this draft)
        2.B.2.B . . . all the same shuttle
Unit 3: 3.B.3.B . . . "   "   "   "
Unit 2: 2.B.2.B . . . "   "   "   "
Followed by A.B.A.B. as desired. Then weave Units 2, 3, and 2 again.
Alternate the plain weaving and the unit weaving as desired for the entire length.

THE LACE BRONSON

An examination of a unit of Point Bronson given on page 143 shows that, if it is repeated over and over again in a draft, long

floats of weft over warp will occur. It was to overcome this that the
Lace Bronson was devised for this variation sacrifices one of the
harnesses, usually the second or the fourth, and uses it for tie-down
threads. The units of Lace Bronson consist of six warp ends instead
of four and at five-thread intervals the weft will be caught by a
tie-down thread, thus eliminating long floats.

Lace Bronson units are as follows:

> Unit 1 . . . 1.2.1.2.1.4 (read from left to right)
> Unit 2 . . . 1.3.1.3.1.4   "   "   "   "   "

Written this way, all the warp ends on harness 4 are the tie-down
threads. It is now possible to repeat a unit as many times as desired
when threading—even for the entire width if desired.

The tie-up is the same as for the Point Bronson except that
treadle number three is not used.

The following is a short draft for a Lace Bronson. Substitute the
correct warp ends for each unit.

COLLIN'S NAPKIN. (ARRANGEMENT BY RUPERT PETERS)

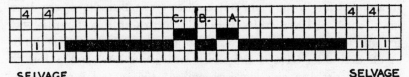

SELVAGE   SELVAGE

Diagram 29.

Thread right-hand selvage.
    "   ten repeats of unit 1.
    "   A–B as desired.
    "   C to balance the design.
    "   ten repeats of unit 1.
    "   left-hand selvage.

The Lace Bronson uses *both* tabby treadles, but like the Point
Bronson the same shuttle is used for both tabby and pattern. For
hems tromp A.B.A.B. etc. End on B.

> For unit 1 tromp as follows: (each shot once) 1 B 1 B A B
> For unit 2   "   "   "   "   "   "   2 B 2 B A B

Both units together: If you would like to weave both units at the
same time, tie up another treadle to harnesses 1, 2 and 3 (sinking

shed) or to harness 4 (rising shed) and use it in place of the pattern treadles of Diagram 27.

The tromping for Collin's napkin follows the units in the draft as follows: Treadle A.B.A.B. etc., for a hem. End on B, then:

Unit 1 . . 10 times for the corner. It should become a square.
Unit 2 . . twice ⎱
Unit 1 . . twice ⎰ Alternate x times for the center
end with:
Unit 2 . . twice
Unit 1 . . ten times for the corner
A.B.A.B. etc. for hem.

Note the B A B shots with which each unit of tromping ends. Where these three rows occur in the weaving, characteristic little "windows" of the Bronson Lace appear. If they fail to show up well on the loom laundering will enhance their beauty.

There are many beautiful drafts for the Bronson Weave written for looms with more than four harnesses.

This is as good a place as any to tell about what I call the "shock treatment" for linen. I am indebted to Irene Beaudin of the Penland School of Handicrafts, Penland, North Carolina, for this very helpful idea. When linen comes off the loom it is stiff and not at all desirable. Give it the shock treatment. First run a row of machine stitching at each raw end of the material to prevent ravelling. Then place the material in a basin and pour over it *boiling* water. Let stand for three minutes. Remove material, and plunge it into *ice cold* water for another three minutes. Make it ice cold—use ice. Repeat these two operations of hot and cold for three times in all. Then roll the linen in an absorbent towel without wringing or creasing the linen in any way. While still damp, iron on both sides with a very hot iron until the material is bone dry. The final ironing should be done on the wrong side of the material, unless you prefer to have it shiny.

The above treatment will soften the fibers of the linen and make them beautiful, as though they had been laundered many times. Mere steam ironing is not nearly as satisfactory.

When hemming linen take care to sew it very firmly with close stitches. No handwoven linen should ever suffer the indignity of being stitched on a sewing machine.

While Lace Bronson is, like the Point Bronson, primarily a weave for linen fiber, it may also be woven of fine wool to make very pretty baby blankets, lacy scarves, stoles, or shawls.

Chapter 16

THE CRACKLE WEAVE

Originating in Jämtland, a province in western Sweden near the Norwegian border, this weave is known over there as *Jämtlandsväv.* When Mrs. Atwater introduced the weave into this country she renamed it *Crackle,* seeing in the woven fabric a resemblance to the crackle of certain pottery glazes and, also, no doubt, fearing for the pronunciation of its original name! However, to me it seems Jämtlandsväv—pronounced according to my Swedish friends, "Yamt-lands (broad "a") vav (long "a") with the accent on the Yamt—would have been better retained than discarded.

In *A Handweaver's Pattern Book,* Marguerite Davison describes this weave as "a series of small twills, three or four threads long." Crackle weave gives much the same effect as a summer and winter but can create it with four harnesses whereas the more intricate drafts for summer and winter weave require many harnesses. Like summer and winter, however, the size of the blocks in the Crackle weave is unlimited for there are never more than three warp ends skipped over by the weft. (There may be fewer than three.) Either side of the material may be regarded as the right side. From all this it can be seen that Crackle has many of the advantages of the summer and winter weave plus some of its own.

It has, however, one big disadvantage which is one reason why so many weavers do not use it more often. It is not easy to thread. There are so many of those little twills Mrs. Davison speaks about that the drafts seem to go up and down like scales on a staff of music. However, careful checking of the draft as one goes along overcomes this difficulty.

Crackle is the hardest of the weaves to write drafts for, but most of us are not usually concerned with this problem.

Crackle's close weave makes it suitable for use for linens, bags, coat material, upholstery, rugs, and other items that receive hard wear. It is simple to weave being tromped, as a rule, like an overshot with a tabby thread. Selvages are threaded to twill as usual. One peculiarity of this weave is that the blocks overlap when they are woven.

In the Crackle weave there are four units or blocks, each unit being threaded on three harnesses as follows: * (Read units from left to right).

Unit A... corresponds to the 1 & 2 combination of Overshot...1.2.3.2
Unit B...   "   " " 2 & 3 combination of   "   ...2.3.4.3
Unit C...   "   " " 3 & 4   "   "   "   ...3.4.1.4
Unit D...   "   " " 1 & 4   "   "   "   ...4.1.2.1

In place of giving you a draft for a Crackle, let us transpose the well known Overshot draft for Honeysuckle into the Crackle weave by direct substitution. As an exercise, transposing one weave into another can be great fun, but not always will the result be satisfying. In the case of Honeysuckle however it is, for Honeysuckle Crackle is well liked by most weavers.

First we will take the Honeysuckle draft as given on page 121 and encircle it to find the tromping combinations as was done on that page.

---

* Sometimes the units are written using different harness combinations from these, but the results are the same, provided the tromping is consistent.

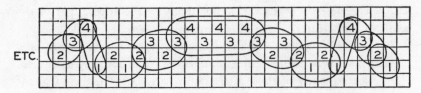

Diagram 10.

Now we will substitute the corresponding Crackle units for each of the Overshot blocks in the circles. When this has been done, we get into trouble right away, for when the Crackle units are written down one after the other in the order required, we know that if the draft were left in that condition there would be 1 & 3 and 2 & 4 combinations and also duplicate harness numbers. As in the Overshot weave, these things are not possible in the Crackle. Nor can there be in a Crackle a block made up of more than three threads. Anything like 3.4.3.4 or 1.2.1.2 in the draft must not occur.

In order to avoid these things, we must insert in between these errors a single warp end threading. Given below is the draft for Honeysuckle Crackle completely worked out. Note where the single warp end threadings have been inserted. In each case the threading inserted is the only possible one that could have been used to correct the error as you can see for yourself. In parentheses above the Crackle units, the corresponding Overshot blocks have been in-

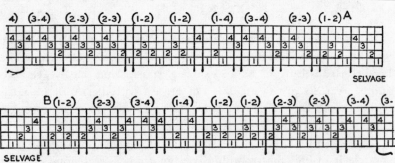

Diagram 30. Honeysuckle Crackle. Thread first 4 warp ends. Then repeat from A to B as desired (B ends on a 2). End with the last 5 warp ends. When the first staff row has been threaded, begin over at the right-hand side of the next one.

dicated. They are merely for comparison and have nothing to do with the threading. Our simple 26-thread repeat has now assumed formidable proportions!

After you have studied this draft, begin with the original Overshot draft and try it yourself. You may never again have occasion to do any more of this, but as an exercise it is not only fun but profitable. There can be more than three "C" units in the center of this draft if desired.

A Crackle draft may be woven in a number of different ways. Here are a few suggestions:

1. In the Overshot Manner: This is the method used in Scandinavia and the one we usually try first. Two shuttles are used, one with a weft for tabby and one with color. For each unit, use only the major harness combination in that unit. For instance, Unit A has two harness combinations. One is composed of the two warp ends on harnesses 1 & 2 and the other of three warp ends (2.3.2). (Note warp end common to both.) The three-threads on harnesses 2 & 3 form the major combination. Thus, to weave Unit A, use treadle 2 (harnesses 2 & 3). For Unit B use treadle 5; Unit C, treadle 6 and Unit D treadle 1. Tromp the units in order as they appear in the draft as many times each as desired for one variation, then you can experiment with the tromping in any way you like.

2. As an Overshot on Opposites: Weave as above but follow one unit's tromping with another which does not have a harness in common. For instance, weave Unit A (2 & 3) as desired then change to Unit C (1 & 4). Similarly Unit B (3 & 4) would be followed by Unit D (1 & 2). Use tabby as usual.

3. As a Summer and Winter: Weave both treadlings in each unit. Unit A would then be woven as follows (use tabby between shots):

Harnesses 1 & 2 (tr. 1)...once
"   2 & 3 (tr. 2)...once
"   1 & 2 (tr. 1)...once
"   2 & 3 (tr. 2)...once

This corresponds to the "Singles" method as described for summer and winter weave on page 135. Crackle units may also be woven as "doubles." And then the treadling for Unit A would be: Tr. 1,2,2,1 with a tabby before and after each pattern shot. For the other units, substitute the correct treadles. This method is most effective when using a coarse pattern thread and a fine tabby. It produces a rather indefinite pattern and is suitable for upholstery and for fabrics where you do not desire a too-pronounced figure.

4. In the Italian Manner: This is particularly effective for a drapery material because it produces an unusual texture, drapes well, and permits greater play of color. Two colors may be used but three are better. Due to the blending of colors, the impression is given of having used four colors. Directions for weaving in the Italian manner are given in the discussion of the Overshot weave on pages 128–130.

Of all the Crackle drafts the Honeysuckle is probably the best known. Mrs. Mary Atwater has given us a list of what she considers to be the best Overshot patterns for transposing into Crackles and mentions Blazing Star, Double Bowknot and the Sunrise patterns. Crackle drafts which have been published from time to time in various publications are: Rain-on-the-River, Drifting Shadows, and Three Twills. Mrs. Marguerite Davison's book already mentioned has many small Crackle drafts in it; and the Shuttle Craft Guild has also published several bulletins on this weave.

Chapter 17

PERSONALIZED DESIGN*

There is no better way, it seems to me, to understand weaving and weaving drafts than to set about to make a draft yourself. Thanks to Mrs. Nona Pfeiffer of San Diego, California, this is easier than it sounds.

A name draft, or *Personalized Design,* as Mrs. Pfeiffer calls it, is a simple way to originate a weaving draft by using the letters of one's own name. While it is quite possible that the draft you make this way may already be on record, the method, nevertheless, has led you to do it on your own.

My name draft was worked out for me by Mrs. Pfeiffer. When woven it turned out to be a very pretty little allover pattern to which I have given the name of "Crossed Swords." Here is the way it was done:

On squared paper (about eight to the inch) the letters of my name were printed, beginning at the center of the page. Between each letter a square was skipped and the name was written first to the right and then to the left.

Next, Mrs. Pfeiffer substituted numerals for the letters in the

* Used by permission of Mrs. Nona Pfeiffer.

name. For this the alphabet was divided among the four harnesses as follows:

ABCDEFG ....Harness 1
HIJKLMN ....Harness 2
OPQRSTU ....Harness 3
VWXYZ ....Harness 4

The above substitutions of harnesses for letters were made by writing the numbers down under the letters as follows:

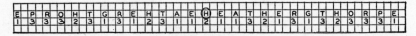

Diagram 31.

In order to correct the resulting figures, the following formula was used:

Between 1 & 1 draft a 4   Where 1 & 3 come together, draft a 4
Between 2 & 2   "   " 3   Where 2 & 4   "   "   "   " 3
Between 3 & 3   "   " 2   Where 3 & 1   "   "   "   " 2
Between 4 & 4   "   " 1   Where 4 & 2   "   "   "   " 1

These insertions were made on the right half of the name draft only, starting at the right. Then Mrs. Pfeiffer made the left side of the draft exactly the same as the right, balancing it from the center outwards after which the figures looked like this:

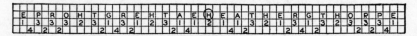

Diagram 32.

Starting at the right hand side, the figures in the two rows shown above were copied down on squared paper in the order in which they came.

Accompanying this chapter is the completed draft of "Crossed Swords." At the top from A to B is one repeat of the draft. When A to B has been threaded as many times as needed, add the last warp end on harness 1 to balance the design. While the selvages have not been indicated, they would be threaded to twill as usual (see page 66). The tie-up, except for the tabby treadles which are tied up to harnesses 1 & 3 and 2 & 4, is shown at the top right. Under the tie-up the x's indicate the tromping. For instance to weave this small overshot pattern, begin as follows: Use a tabby before and after each pattern shot.

> Harnesses 1 & 4 (tr. 6, page 78) once
> " 3 & 4 " 5 " " once
> " 2 & 3 " 2 " " 7 times
> " 1 & 2 " 1 " " once
> etc.

DRAFT OF "CROSSED SWORDS"...A PERSONALIZED DESIGN

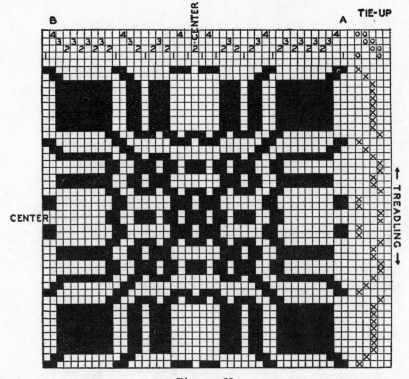

Diagram 33.

Under the draft appears the "draw-down" showing how this draft looks when woven as the tromping indicates. There are numerous flecks of weft which are only one-thread skips over the warp. These are not indicated on the draw-down which is, of course, much larger than the pattern appears when woven. Six-strand floss or #5 pearl cotton makes a nice weft for this small overshot.

Naturally you can use any combinations of words to make a Personalized Design. Perhaps the name of an institution in which you are interested, or the summer home, or your city and street address, or even the dog's name may be the one to start you off on your own personal weaving adventure!

GLOSSARY

ACCIDENTALS—Threadings found in drafts which are necessary to preserve the character of the weave but which are not usually used in the weaving.

APRONS—Lengths of canvas or similar heavy material fastened at one end to the warp and cloth beams of a loom. The other end is hemmed and through the hem an *apron stick* is slipped. The purpose of an apron is to save warp yarn when it is being tied on to the apron stick.

BARGELLO—Embroidery done on canvas. The finished work resembles pointed flames.

BEAM—BREAST BEAM: That part of the loom which is in front of the weaver seated at the loom and over which the woven material passes.

CLOTH BEAM: From the breast beam the woven material passes down and is wound around this beam. Sometimes referred to as FRONT BEAM.

WARP BEAM: The rear beam of the loom upon which the warp is wound. Sometimes referred to as REAR BEAM.

SECTIONAL BEAM: A warp beam divided by pegs or dowels into small sections, usually two inches wide, around which the warp is wound section by section.

PLAIN BEAM: A warp beam which is not divided into sections.

READY-SPOOLED WARP BEAM: A steel hexagonal beam upon which spools of yarn purchased already wound may be placed.

BEAMING—(Verb) Winding a warp on to the beam of a loom.

BEATER—A movable part of the loom which not only beats the weaving into place but also supports the reed. Also called BATTEN.

BINDER ROW—Same as tabby row but specifically a row of plain weave inserted before and after the pattern rows of weaving.

BLOCK—(Noun) A unit of threading.

BOBBIN—A tube or spool upon which weft is wound. It may be made of various materials: paper, wood, plastic, tubular metal. Olden bobbins were made of goose quills. Also called QUILL.

BOBBIN WINDER—An accessory for winding bobbins.

BOUND WEAVING—Weaving in such a manner that the warp is entirely covered on both sides of the material by the floats of weft.

BOUT—A group of warp ends tied on to an apron stick.

BOWKNOT—A looped knot as used to tie a shoe lace.

BRAKE—That part of a loom which helps to put tension on the warp beam. A loom does not necessarily need to have a brake. See Ratchet.

BRAKE TIE—A temporary tie made around the entire warp after the winding on the frame or reel is completed and before it is removed. Its purpose is to prevent snarls from going any farther when the warp is being spread preparatory to beaming. Also called the CHOKER.

CARPET WARP—Heavy cotton yarn used especially for a warp when weaving rag rugs, but which may also be used advantageously as weft, both for tabby and pattern shots. Carpet warp may be 8/3 or 8/4, usually the latter.

CHAINING—Removing a warp from warping frame or reel by a method similar to crocheting.

CORD—Any small-sized, but strong rope of cotton or linen used to tie up treadles, lamms, harnesses, rollers, etc., of a loom.

COUNT—A system of numbering used to designate the thickness (grist) of any thread. Also, specifically, a unit of measurement for worsted yarns which measures 560 yards single-ply.

COVERLET—Another word for bedspread. Also: coverlid, cover, *kivver*.

CRACKLE—One of the weaves for a four-harness loom, so called because of the resemblance of its texture to the crackle of certain pottery glazes. Syn: Jämtlandsväv.

CREEL—A rack for holding tubes or spools of warp. Same as SPOOL RACK.

CROSS—(Noun) A means of separating the warp ends for purposes of counting them and to facilitate and make possible the spreading and threading of the warp. A warp may be prepared with two crosses: the first or *porrey* cross and the second or *portee* cross. When two crosses are made, the portee cross is put on the warp beam first.

CROWDING—Putting more than the required number of warp ends in a dent of the reed. May be done deliberately to produce a desired effect, but more often an error in the sleying.

CUT—A term used to designate the count of wool. Equivalent to 300 yards.

DENIER—A unit used to designate the count of various yarns, especially rayon.

DENT—An opening in the reed through which the ends of the warp are put. The more dents a reed has per inch of its length, the finer the material which may be woven with it. Often more than one warp end is put through each dent of a reed.

DOG—A catch or pawl of a ratchet.

DOUBLES—A term used when referring to one of the methods of weaving the summer and winter weave in which the pattern shots are woven in pairs. Hence, synonymous with IN PAIRS.

DOUP—The long loop at each end of a string heddle.

DOWELS—Cylindrical wooden rods which may be purchased in a wide range of diameters.

DRAFT—Any weaving pattern.

DRAW-DOWN—(Noun) A method of showing on squared paper how a draft would appear if woven.

FABRIC—A term used to denote any woven material.

FIBER—The material of which a thread is made, such as cotton, linen, wool, etc. Also used when referring to the thread itself.

FILLING—A synonym for weft but more often used in commercial weaving than handweaving.

FINISHING—(Noun) 1. The laundering of fabrics. 2. More specifically, with regard to woolens and worsteds, the final process after the material is taken from the loom. It frequently consists of a short laundering in mild suds after which the material is dry cleaned or merely steam pressed. See also FULLING.

FLANGE—A rim such as that found at the end of a spool.

FLAT—An error which appears in fabric caused by a misthreading of the draft. Sometimes, however, a flat is deliberately threaded for the effect, and sometimes it is due to the character of the weave.

FLOAT—A skip of the weft over the warp ends. Syn: Overshot, Weft skip.

FLY SHUTTLE—A shuttle which is not touched by the hand of the weaver during the process of weaving but is either automatic as in the case of industrial weaving on power looms or is impelled by means of a pull on a cord on a hand loom.

FRICTION BRAKE—A brake used instead of a ratchet on the warp beam. It permits a very fine adjustment of the tension on the warp, and consists of a steel band which encircles the beam. The loom shown in the Frontispiece of this book has such a brake but, unfortunately, it does not show in the photograph.

FULLING—(Noun) A process by which woven materials are thickened or *fulled* before they are made into garments by heating, moistening, and pressing. One who fulls is called a *fuller*.

GAUGE—A standard measure, used in the sense of the thickness of a metal.

GRIST—Thickness of yarn. Count of yarn.

HANDTREE—The upper horizontal part of the beater, grooved at the lower edge which rests upon the reed. Sometimes there is a handle in the middle of the handtree.

HANDWOVEN—Most handweavers distinguish between fabrics woven on a loom equipped with a fly shuttle and one which is strictly a hand loom and without any device for throwing the shuttle. Materials woven on a loom with a fly shuttle they refer to as *hand loomed* while those woven with a hand-propelled shuttle they refer to as *handwoven*.

HANK—This term usually refers to a unit of worsted yarn containing 560 yards. A hank of 1/1 cotton yarn, however, contains 840 yards.

HARNESS—A term used in this book to indicate a single frame of a loom upon which the heddles are strung. Hence, often called a *heddle frame*. More correctly the word *harness* refers to all the heddle frames complete with rollers, cords, etc., taken together, but this usage, common in Great Britain, has never found much favor among handweavers in the United States.

HEADING—A few rows of tabby weaving at the beginning or end of a piece of weaving as for a hem. A heading of very heavy weft is used on a new warp to spread it ready for weaving.

HEDDLE—One of a set of cords or wires having an eye through which a warp end is threaded. There are various types. Some are made of flat steel wire, some of round wire and some of string. *Repair heddles* are metal heddles which can be snapped onto the harness and inserted wherever needed in order to correct an error in the threading.

HEEL BAR—That part of the loom which is in front at the floor level or where the heels of the weaver come when the treadles are operated.

HERRINGBONE—A derivative of the twill weave in which the direction of the diagonals changes according to the draft.

HORSES—An arrangement for hanging the harnesses of a loom.

HUCKABACK—A strong fabric, usually of linen, much used for toweling originally, but now used for table linens and all manner of other handwoven materials.

Also a four-harness weave. Syn: Huck.

IRREGULAR TIE-UP—A system of tying up the treadles of a loom so that some or all of the harnesses operate either one by one or more than two at a time.

ITALIAN MANNER—A method of rotating the order in which shuttles are used for color effects in pattern weaving.

JACKS—Levers which are found above or below the harnesses and which, being connected to them, cause the harnesses to rise when the treadles are operated.

LAMMS (LAMS)—Horizontal levers between the treadles and the harnesses by means of which the former are tied indirectly to the harnesses. A four-harness loom has four lamms.

LEA—A varying measure of yarn. A lea of linen contains 300 yards.

LEASE (LEASH) STICKS—Two smooth, thin, flat sticks inserted in the warp to preserve the cross. They have holes drilled at each end so that they can be tied together.

LEVER, HAND—A mechanism by which the harnesses of a table loom are raised and lowered again by hand. Hand levers are numbered from the front to the rear of the loom.

LONG-STAPLED—A term used to designate a long fiber of raw wool or cotton.

LOOM—Any frame for stretching a warp upon which weaving can be done. There are various kinds of looms, such as:

VERTICAL: An upright loom used chiefly in tapestry weaving. Navajo Indian looms are also vertical.

TABLE: A loom without treadles. They are usually narrower than floor looms and placed upon a table. Treadle attachments may be purchased for such looms.

JACK TYPE: A loom equipped with jacks to raise the harnesses when the treadles are in use. Syn: Jack action.

COUNTERBALANCED: One in which the harnesses are balanced in pairs so that when two harnesses are drawn down by the operation of a treadle or treadles, the other two rise.

FLOOR: Any loom that operates by treadles no matter how many harnesses it has or what type.

ONE-SHUTTLE WEAVE—A weave which uses only one shuttle. If there is a tabby or binder row to be woven, the same shuttle is used as for the pattern rows.

OPPOSITES—Refers to the harnesses. The two front harnesses are the opposites of the two rear ones. The two inner ones are the opposites of the two outer. Weaving *on opposites* makes use of these combinations.

OVERSHOT—A skip made by the weft over the warp. Same as float or weft skip. Also a weave whose beauty is due to these skips.

PADDLE—A small rectangular piece of wood, with or without a handle, perforated with two vertical rows of holes and used in the preparation of a warp.

PATTERN—A design or a weaving draft.

PICK—A single throw of the shuttle carrying weft through the shed. Syn: row, shot.

PLAIN WEAVE—A weave in which the shuttle passes over and under the warp ends one by one as in darning. Same as tabby.

PLY—(Verb) To twist or spin two or more strands of a fiber together. (Noun) Used in combination with figures to denote how many strands have been spun together as: 2-ply, 3-ply, or 20/2 (two strands of a number 20 fiber), etc.

PROFILE—Same as short draft.

QUILL—Another word for bobbin.

RADDLE—A rake-like part (minus the handle) used to spread the warp while it is being wound on the plain beam of a loom. Some raddles are made to fit into the beater, taking the place temporarily of the reed. Others have a grooved and usually hinged top which can be lowered over the pegs so that the warp ends cannot come out. Used for spreading the warp while it is being beamed.

RATCHET—A wheel having teeth inclined in one direction and equipped with a catch called a *dog* or *pawl* which puts tension on the front and rear beams of a loom and enables the weaver to move the warp forward as weaving progresses.

REED—That part of a loom which spaces the warp ends evenly. The reed also governs the width of the material and forms part of the beater.

REED OR DRAW-IN HOOK—1. A long-handled hook which may be used either for threading the warp ends or for sleying them through the dents of the reed.

2. Also a smaller hook which has no handle and is shaped something like the letter "s." This type of hook is used for sleying only.

REEL—A piece of weaving equipment used when winding (preparing) a warp.

REPEAT—(Noun) The unit which is necessary to complete one pattern and which is repeated as many times as indicated or desired.

RISING SHED—An opening formed in the warp when the harnesses rise by means of jacks or other type levers. Opposite of *sinking shed.* Table looms and jack type or jack action looms have rising sheds.

ROLLERS—Long horizontal rods from which the harnesses of a loom are frequently hung, usually by means of cords. A four-harness loom requires one large roller and below it two smaller ones for the suspension of its harnesses.

ROSE FASHION—A method of weaving an overshot pattern without diagonals.

RUN—A unit measurement of woolen yarns. A run of No. 1 single-ply woolen yarn measures 1600 yards and weighs one pound.

SELVAGE—Outside edges of the material. Usually four extra warp ends are threaded at each side of a warp to be the selvages for without them the first and last part of the pattern threading would be lost by the drawing-in that is bound to occur in the weaving. Also *selvedge.*

SETT—Closeness with which the warp ends are sleyed through the dents of the reed. Example: Sett, 30 ends to the inch.

SETTING-UP PROCESS—A term used to designate all the steps necessary to getting a warp on a loom and ready for weaving. Synonymous with dressing a loom.

SHED—A wedge-shaped opening made in the warp in front of the reed (though there are also sheds which form behind it and also behind the harnesses). These sheds are formed when a weaver treadles the loom or operates the hand levers. The shuttle with its weft is put through the shed formed in front of the reed.

SHED REGULATOR—An attachment to a loom so constructed that a counterbalanced loom can be used satisfactorily with irregular tie-ups.

SHORT DRAFT—A method of writing drafts in which, to save time and space, only the units of the weave are indicated.

SHOT—A single throw of the shuttle. Syn: row, pick.

SHUTTLE—That which carries the weft thread. There are various types of shuttles which a handweaver uses: flat or stick shuttle around which the weft is wound, a rug shuttle upon which heavy wefts can be carried. Most handweavers, however, use the shuttle called from its shape a *boat shuttle*. With it a bobbin must be used. See also fly shuttle.

SHUTTLE RACE—A narrow, shelflike board attached to the bottom transverse bar of the beater and along which the shuttle glides. Not all looms are so equipped.

SINGLES—A method of weaving a summer and winter draft so that the pattern shots do not come in pairs.

SINKING SHED—A shed which is obtained by drawing down one or more harnesses of a loom. Counterbalanced looms have sinking sheds.

SLABSTOCK—The rear upper horizontal bar of a loom over which the warp passes en route to the warp beam.

SLACK—Loose.

SLEYING—The process of drawing or threading the warp ends through the dents of a reed.

SNITCH OR LOOM KNOT—A knot used when tying treadle, lamm, and harness cords. It does not jam and can be easily adjusted.

SPOOL RACK—A vertical frame with removable, horizontal steel rods or dowels which are slipped through the spools upon which the warp has been wound or purchased. Its purpose primarily is to facilitate the winding of a warp on the warping frame, reel or sectional beam.

SPOT WEAVE—Another name for the Bronson Weave.

SPREADING—Putting the warp ends through a reed or raddle in a temporary sleying. Purpose: to keep the warp at the desired width while it is being beamed on the plain warp beam.

SQUARE COUNT—To weave so that there are as many picks of weaving per inch as there are warp ends per inch in the reed.

SQUARE THE DIAGONAL—When a draft is woven in this way, all the blocks which occur on the diagonal of the design are woven until they are square.

STAR FASHION—A draft which is woven so that there are diagonals which cross in the center of the design is one woven *star fashion*. Opposite of *rose fashion*.

SWIFT—A reel used either for holding hanks or skeins or upon which hanks can be wound.

SYNTHETIC—Man-made. Nylon, rayon, orlon, etc., are synthetic fibers.

TABBY—Plain weave in which the odd-numbered warp ends form one part of the shed and the even-numbered the other.

TABBY SHED: A shed made as above.

TABBY TREADLE: A treadle tied up to weave tabby.

TARTAN—A pattern formed by a regular succession of colors identical in warp and weft and woven in twill.

TAUT—Firm, tightly stretched.

TENSION—State of being stretched with special reference to the amount of strain placed upon a warp while being wound or woven.

TENSIONER—An accessory to a loom by means of which the warp is wound on with even tension. Used in sectional beaming. Syn: Tension box.

TEXTURE—The appearance or character of the woven material. Frequently used to denote a fabric whose beauty is due to the nature and color of warp and weft fibers rather than to any particular pattern.

THREADING—Putting the warp ends through heddles according to a draft.

TIE-DOWN THREADS—Certain warp ends threaded in such a way that they prevent long floats from occurring in the weft.

TIE-UP—The treadles of a loom must be fastened to the lamms and/or the harnesses in a prescribed manner. This is known as the tie-up.

TREADLE—(Noun) That part of the loom operated by the feet. Abbreviation: Tr.

(Verb) To operate a treadle with the feet. Syn: Tromp.

PATTERN TREADLE: A treadle which is not used to weave tabby.

TROMP—A dialectal form of the verb TREADLE.

TROMP AS WRIT—To weave a draft by following the harness combinations as they appear in the draft. Syn: To weave *as drawn in*.

TWILL—A weave. On a four-harness loom twill is usually threaded 4.3.2.1 or 1.2.3.4. In a twill the weft makes diagonals called *wales* across the fabric.

UNIT—A group of warp ends which comprise an integral part of a weave, as for instance, the summer and winter and the M's and O's weaves.

WALE—Diagonal formed in fabric when twill is woven.

WARP—(Noun) The lengthwise threads stretched on a loom.

(Verb) To warp: To put a warp on a loom.

WARP END—A single strand of a warp.

WARP FACE—Having the weft entirely (or almost) covered by the warp so that the pattern appears in the warp. Warp face material is sleyed very closely in the reed.

WARPING FRAME—A wooden framework upon which the warp ends are stretched around pegs or dowels prior to beaming the warp.

WARPING REEL—Same as REEL.

WEAVE—(Verb) To make a fabric by interlacing the warp and weft threads. (Noun) A particular method of threading the warp ends and of weaving with the weft. Ex: Twill, Plain, M's and O's, Bronson, etc.

WEB—The woven part of the warp on the loom.

WEFT—The crosswise threads in the web. The weft is carried in a shuttle when weaving.

WEFT FACE—Material is said to be weft face when the warp is entirely or almost entirely covered by the weft as in BOUND WEAVING. The warp ends must be sleyed much farther apart than in the case of a *warp face* fabric.

WINDING—The process of making or preparing a warp by stretching the warp ends between dowels or pegs on a warping frame or winding them on a warping reel. Sometimes also used with the sense of *beaming*.

WOOF—Synonym for *weft,* and not as commonly used as in the old days.

WORSTED—Hard twisted yarns spun from long-stapled pure wool having its fibers combed so that they lie parallel to one another. Also a mixed yarn so spun.

YARN—Thread of any kind.

BIBLIOGRAPHY

Atwater, Mary Meigs. *The Shuttle-Craft Book of American Hand-Weaving* (rev. ed.). New York: The Macmillan Company, 1951. Colonial handweaving; four to eight harnesses; drafts and their treadling. A text every weaver is proud to own.

————. *Design and the Weaver.* Craft and Hobby Book Service, Pacific Grove, Calif., 1973. The last published work of this author.

Baity, Elizabeth Chesley. *Man Is a Weaver.* New York: The Viking Press, 1942 (out of print). From the first spinners and weavers to the machines of today.

Becher, Lotte. *Handweaving: Designs and Instructions.* How to Do It Series. New York: Studio Publications, 1955 (out of print).

Bériau, Oscar A. *Tissage Domestique.* French text, 1933. *Home Weaving.* English text, 1938 (out of print). Gardenvale, Quebec, Canada: Arts & Crafts of Gardenvale. Especially good on twills.

Black, Mary E. *New Key to Weaving* (13th ed.). New York: The Macmillan Company, 1961. Handweaving techniques and drafts for the beginner as well as much valuable general information. Two to eight harnesses.

Blumenau, Lili. *The Art and Craft of Hand Weaving.* New York: Crown Publishers, 1955.

Bronson, J. & R. *The Domestic Manufacturer's Assistant and Family Directory in the Arts of Weaving.* Utica, N. Y.: Wm. Williams, 1817. Very rare in the original edition. Reprinted: Charles T. Branford Co., Newton Centre, Mass., 1949 (out of print). Quaint and interesting little volume.

Brooks, Marguerite G. Series 2. *Brooks Bouquet and Other Two-Harness Techniques.* Darien, Conn.: Thread Crafts, 1950 (out of print). Printed on heavy folders, post-card size, with photographed examples of each technique. Complete instructions for Brooks bouquet, leno lace, Danish medallion, inlay. For any loom that can make a tabby shed.

Brown, Harriette J. *Hand Weaving for Pleasure and Profit.* New York:

166

Harper & Row, 1952. A guide to two-harness weaving. Additional information concerning fringes, correction of errors, yarn sizes. Extensive bibliography. Weavers on four harnesses find this valuable also.

Burnham, Harold B. and Dorothy K. *Keep Me Warm One Night.* Toronto, Ontario, Canada: University of Toronto Press in cooperation with the Royal Ontario Museum, 1972. Early weaving in eastern Canada concentrating on bedspreads. Wonderful illustrations.

Chetwynd, Hilary. *Simple Weaving.* New York: Watson-Guptill Publications, 1969. A nice little book suitable for schools.

Coates, Helen. *Weaving for Amateurs.* New York: Harper & Row, 1952. Two to four harnesses, includes spinning and dyeing.

Collingwood, Peter. *The Techniques of Rug Weaving.* New York: Watson-Guptill Publications, 1969. Well done.

Davison, Marguerite P. *A Handweaver's Pattern Book* (rev. ed.). Published by the author. Swarthmore, Pa., 1950 (out of print). Over 200 drafts and 1200 illustrations, all from weaving done by the author. Also discussions. Four-harness weaving.

Davison, Marguerite P. (ed.). *A Handweaver's Source Book.* Published by the editor, 1953 (out of print). Collected patterns from Laura M. Allen, some of which are very old. Four-harness overshot patterns.

Eaton, Allen H. *Handicrafts of the Southern Highlands.* New York: Dover Publications, 1973.

Frey, Berta. *Designing and Drafting for Handweavers.* New York: The Macmillan Company, 1958 (out of print).

———. *Seven Projects in Rosepath.* Published by the author, New York, 1948 (out of print). Shows what can be done on this simple threading.

Gallinger, Osma G. *Joy of Handweaving.* Scranton, Pa.: International Textbook Co., 1950 (out of print). In addition to information about looms, designs, and color, this book contains a chart of thread sizes, appropriate settings, etc.

Held, Shirley E. *Weaving: A Craftsman's Handbook.* New York: Holt, Rinehart & Winston, 1973.

Hess, Katharine P. *Textile Fibers and Their Use* (5th ed.). New York: J. B. Lippincott Co., 1954 (out of print).

Hooper, Luther. *Weaving for Beginners.* London: Sir Isaac Pitman & Sons, 1919 (reprinted 1934, out of print). An older text still in use today.

Hopkins, Giles E. *Wool as an Apparel Fiber.* New York: Rinehart & Company, 1953 (out of print).

House, Florence E. *Notes on Weaving Techniques* (7th rev. ed.). 1954 (out of print). Distributed by Arts Cooperative Service, New York. Notes from lectures. For two to eight harnesses.

Ickis, Marguerite. *Weaving as a Hobby.* New York: Sterling Publishing Co., 1968.

Kirby, Mary. *Designing on the Loom.* Craft and Hobby Book Service, Pacific Grove, Calif., 1973.

Kronke, Grete. *Simple Weaving.* New York: Van Nostrand Reinhold Company, 1973.

Lamprey, L. *The Story of Weaving.* New York: Frederick A. Stokes Company, 1939 (out of print).

Lewis, Ethel. *Romance of Textiles.* New York: The Macmillan Company, 1953 (out of print).

Lewis, Griselda. *Handbook of Crafts.* Newton Centre, Mass.: Charles T. Branford Co., 1960.

Little, Frances. *Early American Textiles.* New York: The Century Company, 1931 (out of print).

Millen, Roger. *Weave Your Own Tweeds.* Swarthmore, Pa.: M. P. Davison, 1948 (out of print). Interesting, amusingly written. Advice on the finishing as well as the weaving of tweeds.

Neher, Evelyn. *Four-harness Huck.* Published by the author. New Canaan, Conn., 1953 (out of print). Just about everything there is to know about huck.

Nelson, Norbert. *Selling Your Crafts.* New York: Van Nostrand Reinhold Company, 1973.

Nye, Thelma M. *Swedish Weaving.* New York: Van Nostrand Rheinhold Company, 1972.

Oelsner, Gustaf Herman. *Handbook of Weaves.* Translated by Samuel Dale. New York: Dover Publications, 1915. For the advanced weaver.

Plath, Iona. *The Craft of Handweaving* (abr. ed.). New York: Charles Scribner's Sons, 1972.

Pritchard, M. E. *Dictionary of Weaving.* New York: Philosophical Library, 1956 (out of print). Definitions of names and terms. Also material on spinning and dyeing. Illustrated. Very helpful.

Regensteiner, Else. *The Art of Weaving.* New York: Van Nostrand Reinhold Company, 1970. Well recommended.

Reichard, Gladys A. *Navajo Shepherd and Weaver.* New York: Dover Publications, 1974.

————. *Spider Woman: A Story of Navajo Weavers and Chanters* (2nd ed. reprint of 1934 ed.). Glorieta, N.M.: Rio Grande Press, 1968.

Rodier, Paul. *The Romance of French Weaving.* New York: Frederick A. Stokes Company, 1931 (out of print).

Roth, E. Ling. *Studies in Primitive Looms.* The Bankfield Museum, Halifax, England, 1918 (reprinted in 1934, out of print).

Shillinglaw, Phyl. *Introducing Weaving.* New York: Watson-Guptill Publications, 1972. Aimed at helping teachers and students who wish to introduce weaving in schools.

Simpson, L. E., and Weir, M. *The Weaver's Craft* (7th ed.). Leicester, England: Dryad Press, 1952. Simple instructions for four-harness weaving.

Tate, Lou. *Weaving Is Fun* (6th ed.). Louisville, Ky.: 1948 (out of print). Spiral bound. Instructions for "hemstitching" on the loom, leno lace, Danish medallion, and other techniques of like nature. Good illustrations and directions are easy to follow.

Thorpe, Azalia Stuart, and Larsen, Jack Lenor. *Elements of Weaving.* Garden City, N.Y.: Doubleday & Company, 1967.

Tidball, Harriet. *The Weaver's Book* (7th ed.). New York: The Macmillan Company, 1973.

Waller, Irene. *Designing with Thread.* New York: The Viking Press, 1973. From thread to fabric.

West, Virginia M. *Finishing Touches for the Handweaver.* Newton Centre, Mass.: Charles T. Branford Co., 1967. A study of finishing touches for the handweaver.

Wilson, Jean V. *Weaving Is for Anyone.* New York: Van Nostrand Reinhold Company, 1967.

———. *Weaving Is Creative.* New York: Van Nostrand Reinhold Company, 1973.

———. *Weaving Is Fun.* New York: Van Nostrand Reinhold Company, 1971.

Worst, Edward F. *Foot-Power Loom Weaving.* Milwaukee: Bruce Publishing Co., 1918 (11th printing 1948, out of print). Four to sixteen harnesses. A standard text. Clearly drawn specifications for a loom and accessories. Excellent discussion of double weaves on multiple harness looms. Many drafts and illustrations.

Zielinski, S. A. *Encyclopaedia of Handweaving.* New York: Funk & Wagnalls, 1959. Most useful.

Znamierowski, Nell. *Step by Step Weaving.* Golden Craft Series. New York: Western Publishing Company, 1967 (paperback, 1973).

PERIODICALS, BULLETINS, PAMPHLETS

American Fabrics. Quarterly. A magazine for the trade, but also of interest to handweavers, especially those interested in keeping up to date on styles and color trends. Doric Publishing Co., 24 East 38th St., New York, N.Y. 10016.

Handweaver & Craftsman. Quarterly. 220 Fifth Ave., New York, N.Y. 10001.

Shuttle, Spindle and Dyepot. Handweavers Guild of America, 1013 Farmington Ave., West Hartford, Conn. 06107.

Warp & Weft. Robin and Russ Handweavers, 533 North Adams St., McMinnville, Ore. 97128.

BOOK SUPPLIERS

The Book Barn. P. O. Box 245, Storrs, Conn. 06268.

Craft and Hobby Book Service. Pacific Grove, Calif. Now wholesalers only.

The Unicorn. Box 645, Rockville, Md. 20851. Seymour & Helene Bress. In addition to handling books they also publish an excellent annotated price list and catalog, 25¢.

INDEX

(Pages on which Illustrations and Diagrams will be found are in boldface type.)